FAST BREAK SPORTS

SPORTS MEDIA HANDBOOK

First Edition

By Sue Carter and Dan Krier
Michigan State University

cognella®
academic publishing

Bassim Hamadeh, CEO and Publisher
Michael Simpson, Vice President of Acquisitions
Jamie Giganti, Managing Editor
Jess Busch, Graphic Design Supervisor
John Remington, Acquisitions Editor
Brian Fahey, Licensing Associate
Mandy Licata, Interior Designer

First published in the United States of America in 2015 by Cognella, Inc.

Printed in the United States of America

ISBN: 978-1-63189-070-3 (pbk)/ 978-1-63189-071-0 (br)

www.cognella.com   800-200-3908

Dedicated with thanks to grandsons Benjamin and Harrison, great sports fans; wonderful parents Herman and Marion Krier; and devoted researcher and friend Abbie Newton.

Contents

Introduction   v

Chapter 1

History of Sports, Part I   1

Chapter 2

History of Sports, Part II   7

Chapter 3

History of the Olympics   15

Chapter 4

International Sports   23

Chapter 5

Racial Barriers   31

Chapter 6

Women's Involvement in Sports and Its Coverage   39

Chapter 7

Amateur Athletics in the United States   47

Chapter 8

Sports Media Ethics   55

Chapter 9

The Business Side
of Sports   63

Chapter 10

Sports Agents, Endorsements, and Advertising   71

Chapter 11

Sports Films Throughout the Ages   79

Chapter 12

The Future of Sports Media   89

References   95

Image Credits   111

Introduction

Welcome to *Fast Break Sports: Sports Media Handbook*! As the title suggests, this work is meant to provide easy access to the world of sports and the media in a way that connects the past with the present while offering a look at where things are headed in the immediate future. The last few years have seen an explosion of technological innovation, Internet convergence, and digital expansion. These changes have reshaped the sports media landscape and have increased the popularity of athletic broadcasting and news coverage. Simply put, sports have never before been so comprehensively available for mediated consumption—at home or on the go via the ever-present smartphone—and the dollar values associated with the teams, leagues, and collegiate conferences, and the media that shadow their every move, have never seen such astounding heights.

This book is a wide-ranging reference guide to the history of athletics and the media that cover them. The following chapters are a valuable resource not only for those just beginning to learn about the inseparable bond between sports and the media, but also for those individuals who are already quite familiar with sports media and are seeking a refresher of this information or hoping to fill any gaps in their existing knowledge.

The central goal of this text is to summarize the most important sports milestones, especially those regarding women's rights and the breaking down of racial barriers, while incorporating the ever-increasing omnipresence of the media with regard to the coverage of athletic events. The mission of *Fast Break Sports: Sports Media Handbook* is to illustrate the enormous extent to which sports needs the media and vice versa, for without one another, neither would have expanded into the massive billion-dollar businesses that they now represent in the United States and throughout the world. It is indisputable that sports and the media have never been bigger or more relevant in societies around the globe, whether the content is accessed online, via television or the radio, or through feature films hitting theaters or debuting on network programming. Peoples' psychological well-being and how much they value their culture are indelibly attached to the teams in their respective countries, states, and communities, especially because of the emphasis on participating with honor and integrity in a way that represents the public in a decent and righteous fashion.

Yes, winning matters, but sports mean so much more than a single victory or championship. Sports journalism details the stories that affect communities from the inside out, telling tales of individual triumph, team unity, or overcoming insurmountable odds in ways that teach lessons and remind us of what is truly important about giving your all regardless of the outcome. The inspirational aspects of sports are what lie at the heart of their popularity, and it is through the media that athletic glory is chronicled and immortalized for the remainder of time. It is important to know the specifics of sporting past so that one can understand and appreciate the history that is being made on a daily basis in so many of the different types of athletics occurring around the world.

1

History of Sports, Part I

Ancient History of Sports

Giving an exact date as to when sports "began" is impossible, but there is little doubt that sporting competition has existed and evolved over thousands of years of human history. For instance, the presence of wrestling can be seen in ancient cave drawings dating back to 3400 BCE, which fosters the assumption that athletic competition grew out of a natural human need to exhibit strength and courage. Humans subsequently found sporting events a perfect representation of personal achievement and prowess in skills necessary for survival, as sports could symbolically depict the actions that were involved in deathly wars between tribes, states, and empires.

There are other reasons that sports have evolved as human civilization has progressed. In earlier centuries, skills needed to secure food through hunting were vital for survival. Similarly it is easy to see the development of competitions such as archery, horsemanship and the use of the javelin as rooted in emulations of hunting for the purposes of securing meat for sustenance. Additionally, early sporting events were linked to religious ceremonies. The Olympics in ancient Greece and the Mayan ball game *Ollamaliztli* are examples of athletic competitions affiliated with religious events.

Sports have enabled humans to develop a sense of pride and self-esteem based on athletic ability and accomplishment, feelings that exist to the present day in accordance with victory and winning championships. This notion of more perks and less prejudice toward those who triumphed in sporting competition allowed humans to keep score of which groups of people were better at what types of skills, providing a way in which societies could further strengthen in-groups and compare themselves to neighboring opponents or out-groups among them. The historical examination laid out in this chapter is meant to illustrate the components of early human athletic activities that led to the sports rivalries and types of competition that exist throughout the world in the twenty-first century. By studying the history of sports and its representation in various forms of media, this text presents a comprehensive picture of where humans have come from regarding competitive athletics and where we are heading in the future.

The first recorded form of sports dates back to 5200 BCE, when Egyptian citizens participated in a type of bowling known simply as "bowls." Remnants of a large ancient room discovered by Italian anthropologists in 2007 lend credence to the assumption that humans competed in a game that involved rolling balls down a lane into small holes carved into the floor. Surely this initial example can connect present-day humans with the feelings experienced in proving that one could complete a skillful task better than his or her opponent. Competition, it seems, is an innate human characteristic, and it appears that, for at least the past several thousand years, civilized humans have had a natural predisposition for sports and athletic events.

From the time of ancient Egyptian bowling, the chronology of historical athletic progression has a timeline dotted with a multitude of ever-expanding examples, with instances growing exponentially more frequent as time has moved closer to the present day. As was mentioned earlier, cave paintings from 3400 BCE were discovered in the Nile Valley of Beni Hasan that showed two individuals engaged in a wrestling match. Documentation shows that kung fu began in the Eastern Hemisphere around 2600 BCE. Board games such as those related to backgammon were found in Egyptian culture in 2500 BCE (known as the "Royal Game of Ur"), where sticks were thrown instead of dice.

Cave paintings from 2000 BCE portray humans throwing spears, running and competing, illustrating signs of the establishment of sports in everyday culture. Greek murals from 1520 BCE show men in fighting stances wearing what appear to be boxing gloves. Chariot races featuring harnessed horses and rolling carts began in ancient Egypt circa 1500 BCE, with rowing racing on the Nile River becoming mainstream around 1400 BCE. Other examples of historic sports involve the game of hurling, invented in Ireland in 1272 BCE, as well as tlachtli, a court-based ball game where Aztec men played to the death, which took place in Mesoamerica around 1000 BCE.

The first-ever recorded instances of sportswriting appeared in Homer's two majestic Greek literary classics, the *Odyssey* and the *Iliad*, which were constructed sometime between 800 and 725 BCE and included the outcomes of boxing and wrestling matches in detail. In the stories, Odysseus competed for honor in sporting events that were both religious and competitive in order to prove his value as a man. Sports were also a part of the funeral ceremonies of Achilles' favorite companion, Patroclus, during the Trojan War, once again combining religion with athletics.

Although its roots can be traced back to 1300 BCE, perhaps the most significant institution in the history of sports was officially created in 776 BCE Greece in the city of Olympia to honor Zeus, the father of the Greek gods. Hence, the Olympic Games were established as the paradigm of unified athletic competition, and ushered in the tradition of holding such comprehensive events once every four years beginning with the initial Olympiad. The games served as a measure of strength and honor, and such virtues as health and livelihood became embedded in the culture and were emulated in the form of paintings, sculptures, and lifestyle. The first Olympic Games were held for just one day, and included foot races of two hundred meters, representing the types of customs enacted during solemn occasions like funerals.

As time went on, more events were incorporated into the Olympics, such as different types of running races, javelin throwing, jumping, boxing, wrestling, and chariot and horse racing, all of which were seen in early seventh century BCE records. In the year 708, the pentathlon was added, and in 688, the sport of boxing took place, with fighters wearing leather swaths around their wrists and knuckles instead of padded gloves covering their whole hands. Starting in 652 BCE, a dangerous sport named pankration was introduced to the Olympics, and this no-rules precursor to mixed martial arts fighting involved bouts that ended only when one combatant acknowledged a loss or suffered death. Oftentimes, the lone result was the killing of an opponent who would never risk the disgrace of tarnished family pride from a voluntary admission of defeat.

The sport of polo, wherein men on horses use clubs to swat balls on a field, much like a game of hockey, was created in Persia in the year 525 BCE and was used as a form of training for war and military expertise. Stitchings of this majestic competition were commonly heralded on tapestry. Such was the nature of ancient sports, with their foundations linked to the ideals of pride, survival, and strength in battle. Perhaps the most notorious celebrated story involving such a combination of athletic prowess and belligerence was the marathon, that sprang from a 490 BCE war between the Greeks and Persians. According to ancient lore, a messenger was sent on foot from the Greek city of Marathon to the capital of Athens to deliver news of the impending defeat of the enemy so that preparations could be made to finish off the Persians. This unnamed runner collapsed and died after conveying the message, and the legend of the marathon was born, forever commemorated in a race that honored the 26.2-mile distance of the fateful informant.

Soccer, or football as the rest of the world refers to it, was first concocted by the Chinese in 206 BCE in the form of a game called "tsu chu," or "cuju." Again, this sport was developed as a military exercise to teach warriors structure and teamwork. At around the same time, a type of football or rugby called "Haxey Hood" was played in Lincolnshire, England, wherein men competed for the reward of free alcoholic beverages by pushing a leather tube towards the opponent's zone. To this day, the English celebrate more than seven hundred years of heritage based on this competition, alcohol and merriment included.

For American tastes, the sport of harpastum was developed by Romans in the first century BCE, and this game is believed to be the ancestor of American football. Requiring the attributes of speed, strength, and agility, players on teams were given the task of carrying a hard, softball-sized object toward the other squad in hopes of advancing their position at all costs. By progressing over a goal line by running, throwing, or kicking the ball, harpastum players scored points for their side, thus laying the groundwork for future sports mainstays rugby and American football. One last note on harpastum was the lack of rules associated with the game. It was a win-at-all-costs endeavor, only for the most courageous of the day: a fact that still exists in present times.

To finish out athletics before the modern calendars began counting up instead of down, it is worth considerable note that Japanese sumo wrestling saw its inception in the year 23 BCE. The first champion went by the name of Nomi no Sukune, and he is now known in historical records as the patron saint of sumo.

The early first century CE saw the advent of such games as marbles in England, which was shown to the inhabitants by the Romans. Second-century Greeks and Romans squared off in a nascent form of volleyball known as "episkyros," wherein a ball was thrown back and forth over a high-strung netting. Finally, athletic competitions dealing with the prowess of aiming a bow and arrow were first recorded by third-century Europeans, thus beginning the era of archery that continues across the globe today.

For those anxious about whether or not board games should be considered athletic events, let us not leave out the skillfulness of the mind, especially when it comes to a pursuit as strategically intellectual and consequential as chess. The game of chess was established as commonplace in sixth-century Persia, going by the name of "shah mat," or "the king is dead," which became the present-day proclamation of "checkmate." This test of brilliance was meant to aid in military tactics, and it quickly garnered a worldwide devotion to the point that it became an international competition. Other board games from similar times included igo, a Japanese creation that works much like the skill game Othello, and dominoes, which was invented by the Chinese in the ninth century. During this time, playing cards were also developed and found their way toward Europe, where the suits of hearts, clubs, spades, and diamonds were eventually affixed to form the modern decks we have been familiar with for centuries.

To continue the theme of skill, in eleventh-century France, a game known as "jeu de paume" became the first exhibition of what we all recognize as tennis. Tournament jousting also saw its creation at the same time in 1066 in England, and bullfights were publicly announced in 1080 in Spain. In the twelfth century, ice skating began as a competitive event in the Fenlands of England, and in the year 1300, the game of cricket was born, shaping the form of the popular sport played around the world today. In the sixteenth century, the game of billiards became popular in France as a recreation of affluence, and competitive swimming was introduced to Japanese schools in the year 1603.

Pertaining to rules and regulations, it wasn't until the year 1618 that the King James *Book of Sports* was printed to describe legitimate and courteous competitions allowed in England. Football, for some reason, was not considered one of the noble athletic events worthy of inclusion in such a book.

As the seventeenth and eighteenth centuries progressed in Europe, dozens of sporting events that we know as ordinary today sprang up and found favor with the masses. The first steeplechase race was run in Ireland in 1752, fencing was founded in 1754, the first American regatta was recorded in 1756, the *Sportsman's Dictionary*—a first—was printed in 1778, and the sport of baseball was mentioned in 1798 by author Jane Austen in her book *Northanger Abbey*.

In the nineteenth century, athletics saw a boom in interest and participation as information was able to be transferred more easily around the globe. The first gymnasium was built in 1817 in the U.S. Army Military Academy in West Point, New York, and the first rowing championships were held in England in 1831. The year 1840 saw the advent of ski jumping in Europe, and in 1841, the U.S. Ski Team was formed. In 1845, global rules for rugby were established to foster cohesion of the sport within the British Empire, and 1846 saw the initial swimming championships held in Sydney, Australia. In 1860, ice hockey was initially played in its modern-day form in Toronto, Canada, and the remainder of the century found golf championships and soccer clubs and leagues springing up all over England. In 1872, the inaugural FA Cup, or Football Association Cup Final, was held in England, a soccer tournament that is still held yearly.

In the United States, arguably, the most popular sports have always been baseball and football, and the nineteenth century was the time in which rules were written down and agreed on for the most part. In 1845, "father of baseball" Alexander Cartwright's rules were first recognized, and 1867 yielded the Princeton Rules of American football, which began to take the safety of the players into account for the first time in football history. In 1870, the Chicago Cubs baseball team was assembled, and in 1871 the National Association of Professional Baseball Players was put together in New York City. Regarding basketball, the game was invented in Springfield, Massachusetts, in 1891, when James Naismith hung peach baskets for a class of students at the local YMCA. Hoping to combine the skills of rugby, lacrosse, and soccer with that of football and hockey, Naismith initially developed thirteen basic rules for the game, nine of which are still enforced today. In other North American firsts of note, the Stanley Cup ice hockey tournament was created in Canada in 1893 and was most likely celebrated with a fistfight between two toothless men.

In the twentieth century, sports continued to expand on the playing field and in households across the country, with games such as Scrabble being invented in 1931. Worldwide, the Fédération Internationale de Football Association, or

FIFA, was formed in 1904, and the first-ever World Cup soccer tournament took place in Uruguay in 1930. In 1924, the first Winter Olympic Games were held in Chamonix, France.

Other tidbits of importance include the start of the Professional Golfers Association, or PGA, in 1901, and the 1911 Indianapolis 500 car race, the first of its kind. The National Hockey League (NHL) was established in 1917, the National Football League (NFL) was formed in 1919, and the National Boxing Association was punched up by its creators in 1920.

It is easy to imagine how sports took hold of the worldwide population as the ability to communicate with others became faster and less costly. Humans have always showed an innate need to express themselves athletically to determine their levels of skill and physical prowess, and the development of such an abundance of sporting events seems like no coincidence when one ponders how involved modern-day humans are with sport scores and future events. People of all ages can compete in almost any type of sport these days, and there is no sign of athletics slowing up any time soon. Only the future knows where sports are headed, but based on this examination of the history of competition over the past several thousand years, it is almost undisputable that sports are not going away anytime soon, if ever.

2

History of Sports, Part II

History of Sports Media

Before discussing the history of sports media, it is imperative to first visit the fundamental turning point of all modern mass media: the invention of the printing press by Johannes Gutenberg in Germany around the year 1440. Before this vital innovation, books were hand-copied by monks and available only to the richest and most prosperous citizens of Europe. Gutenberg's expertise at typography allowed for the development of a machine that could create a template off which any number of copies could be mechanically created and distributed to the masses. Simply put, without the printing press, there would never have been the explosion of ideas that went on to connect global cultures and blur the line between who was privileged enough to read books and magazines and those who were so poor that they were doomed to a life of illiteracy.

Writing, of course, precedes the printing press by thousands of years, with Middle Eastern alphabets dating back to 1900 BCE, continuing on into Greek and Roman cultures as time went on. In 59 CE, Roman emperor Julius Caesar instructed the circulation of a "pamphlet" titled *Acta Diurna*, which reported on significant social and political events of the day to his constituents. These notices were carved on stone or metal and posted in public places around Rome to keep politicians up-to-date on the latest breaking news, if engraved stone can be considered breaking. In 105 CE, Chinese scholars concocted the oldest-known script after the development of paper and ink, along with printing blocks to be used as stamps for the wealthy

and powerful. It was the Koreans in 1234 who created the world's first moveable type, which was subsequently refined in Germany for Gutenberg's grand construction. The rest, as they say, is history, and that history will be examined now.

It didn't take long for religious leaders in Europe to take advantage of the printing press, with the first mass-produced Bible put out in 1455 by the Catholic church. This, not coincidently, greatly increased the literacy rates in the civilized world, and helped usher in a new thirst for ideas and invention that brought about the Renaissance of the late fifteenth century, with geniuses such as Italy's Leonardo da Vinci producing some of humanity's most celebrated print and painted images (e.g., *The Mona Lisa*, *The Last Supper*, and *The Vitruvian Man*).

By the year 1500, more than thirty-five thousand books had been published, and people such as Martin Luther saw fit to put their own personal spin on Christianity, as Luther did with the version of the Bible that he published in 1522. In 1605, the world's first weekly newspaper commenced production in Antwerp, Belgium, and in 1666, the *London Gazette* began to hit the masses by the thousands. America's first newspaper showed up in 1690 in the form of Boston's *Publick Occurrences*, which was published without permission from the overseeing British government. Though this trailblazing American publication was soon shut down, 1704 saw the inception of the *Boston Newspaper*, a heavily regulated weekly that endured closer scrutiny by the colonial overseers.

As the year 1783 came to a newly independent United States of America, forty-three newspapers were officially being published in the former British colonies—journals instrumental in enhancing the communication between American forces during the Revolutionary War. These papers created the backbone of the press in the United States and provided a means of sharing opinions and ideas amongst cities and states. After the ratification of the Bill of Rights in 1791 ensured the freedom of the press that exists to this day, more than 346 newspapers sprang to life during the following fifty years. Without a doubt, these publications helped bring about the American renaissance known as the Industrial Revolution of the late nineteenth century.

During the Industrial Revolution, the mechanized printing presses of American innovation enabled a whopping ten thousand items to be produced every hour, which propelled the number of newspapers past 2,500 by the year 1850 and to more than 11,000 by the year 1880! Though it may seem like a long time ago, the motorized inventions of this time began the push to the ubiquity of the Internet and mass technology that we have in present times, all in the span of under two hundred years. It's truly amazing, especially if one puts into perspective that the first-ever alphabet took more than three thousand years to be able to be copied in another fashion besides the human hand.

In terms of magazine publication, the first to hit British shelves occurred in 1731: an entertainment and news journal called *Gentleman's Magazine*. In the United States, a man in Philadelphia named William Bradford backed the publication of America's first magazine, known as *American Magazine* (leaving one to wonder how on Earth he came up with such a title). Magazines were more of an upper-class mainstay, so their popularity was never destined to rise like that of the lower-priced newspaper. Though the 1800s saw some titles surviving on tabloid-type muckraking, it truly was not until after World War II when magazines soared in popularity, with target-specific titles such as *Ladies Home Journal* and *Popular Mechanics* flourishing and taking the medium to the end of the century.

Sports reporting, on the other hand, was something that found a quick audience with newspaper readers in the early 1700s. On March 5, 1733, the *Boston Gazette* published the first sports story in American history, a summary of an English boxing match copied most likely from a British counterpart. By the 1790s, Americans were used to getting their athletic event news from England's various magazines, but it wasn't until 1819 when a magazine known as the *American Farmer* began publishing news articles about hunting, cycling, and fishing, along with several other topics. Then, in the late 1820s, several magazines in the United States became completely devoted to sports, cover to cover. One well-known example of this was the *Spirit of the Times*, a publication by William Trotter Porter that published schedules, results, and team records. Overall, though, sports carried a negative connotation. Because boxing was more popular with immigrants and the lower economic classes, so many of the newspapers of the day covered only horse racing, given its interest to the wealthy in society. Nonetheless, sports began to gain popularity across the board, and with literacy rates rising, so did the number of publications devoted to the subject.

In the 1840s, Porter's *Spirit of the Times* gained a newfound level of acclaim, bursting to a national circulation of more than 100,000 thanks to its coverage of baseball, which was soon to be known as "America's pastime." The publication made sure to detail and explain the rules of the game, which helped recruit new fans and subsequent readers to the paper. In 1853, the *New York Clipper* was another newspaper that helped bring more attention to baseball, allowing editor Harry Chadwick to garner the moniker "The Father of the Game." During this time span, other newspapers including the *New York Herald*, the *New York Tribune*, and *The New York Times* also came into existence, all allocating a section of print to sports scores and stories.

After the Civil War ended in 1865, baseball far and away grew into the most popular sport in America. National sportswriters championed the health benefits of playing the game, thus spawning a larger interest from families and their children. The perception was to train children to compete in new battles associated with everyday living, and, accordingly, the image of sports overall gained appeal.

An important note on the expansion of sports deals with the electric telegraph, which was developed independently in the United States in the 1830s by Samuel Morse, inventor of the Morse code. By the mid-1850s, a transatlantic cable was laid, enabling communication between continents which ushered in a new era of sports journalism fueled by the fast relays of information between large distances. A seminal example of this occurred in 1867, when the *New York Herald* paid money to broadcast blow-by-blow results of a boxing title match between English fighters Jem Mace and Joe Goss. It wasn't quite high-speed broadband, but it sufficed for those with no other option, as anyone familiar with dial-up Internet as a last resort would agree.

As the nineteenth century came to a close, the United States experienced an unprecedented jump in immigration with the advent of new industrialization, and these factors also led to more people becoming interested in sports as civilian populations swelled around major cities.

The 1920s, without a doubt, will forever be known as the Golden Age of Sports. Writers such as Warren Susman penned that this is "when American infatuation with professional athletics began, giving a virtual coup de grace to religion as the non-economic and non-sexual preoccupation of millions of middle-class Americans." The Roaring Twenties were known for their excesses, and sports became one of the luxuries of everyday life. They provided a source of entertainment as well as a potent cultural component, thanks to baseball superstars such as Babe Ruth, Lou Gehrig, and Ty Cobb. One poll taken in that decade revealed that 80 percent of all American men read the sports section of a newspaper at some point of the week, which likely had much to do with the Associated Press creating its own sports division around that time. In addition, whereas less than 1 percent of newspaper space was allocated to sports in the 1880s, that number jumped to somewhere between 12 and 20 percent by the end of the 1920s. Soon, the desire for more sports media reached such a peak that necessity became the mother of invention, and the birth of the electromagnetic radio took hold of the world.

Like the printing press before it, the radio proved to be the great leap forward for mass media in the twentieth century, especially concerning the dissemination of sporting events to a wide audience. Though the device was invented in its most elementary form in the nineteenth century, radio gained huge popularity in the 1920s as it became available as a home entertainment accessory to families throughout the United States. To give a quick indication of the radio's abundant presence and rapid growth related to home purchase, at the beginning of the decade, merely one in four hundred families possessed a radio of its own, but by 1929 the proportion had changed to one in three. Now a family could sit and listen together on a daily basis, enjoying the thrills of live sports broadcasts such as boxing matches or the sounds of the ballpark with the crack of the bat and the roar of the crowd as a home run sailed through the spring and summer air.

September 6, 1920, will go down in history as the date that sports made its debut on American radio waves. The event was a boxing prize fight between heavyweight champion Jack Dempsey and Billy Miske, with Dempsey scoring a third-round knockout. In November 1920, WTAW in College Station, Texas, locally broadcast the nation's first-ever football game, a contest between Texas University and Mechanical College of Texas. Then, on July 2, 1921, the "Battle of the Century" was fed through the airwaves from Newark, New Jersey's WJZ, announced by Major J. Andrew White, as Jack Dempsey retained his heavyweight crown with a fourth-round knockout of Frenchman Georges Carpentier.

Other sporting highlights regarding the radio in the 1920s included the first-ever baseball game broadcast by Pittsburgh's KDKA on August 5, 1921, with the voice of Harold Arlin spoken through a telephone streamed over the airwaves. Two months later, KDKA called the 1921 World Series between the New York Giants and New York Yankees, with famed sportswriter Grantland Rice providing the play-by-play for all eight of the games. One month later, on November 5, Arlin was back in the radio booth, this time calling the first national college football game ever, a matchup between the Pittsburgh Panthers and the West Virginia Mountaineers. This began a trend wherein college football boomed in mass appeal across the eastern United States. In 1924, Rice referred to Notre Dame's star backfield as the "Four Horsemen," a nickname that still conjures up images of black-and-white photos of the vintage athletic warriors. Finally, on New Year's Day 1926, the very first Rose Bowl game was broadcast via radio to a national audience, and in following years the game was called by Graham McNamee, who some consider to be the greatest radio broadcaster of all time. Just as sports players became stars for their performances on the field, radio sportscasters became well-known personalities for their audible qualities and likable temperaments heard nationwide.

As the twentieth century progressed, sports radio became even more present in American daily life, especially near the end of World War II, with regular broadcasts such as Gillette's *Cavalcade of Sports* created in 1944. The growth trend continued with the invention of the transistor radio in 1954, which allowed for the handheld gadget to travel anywhere on battery power, enabling sports fans across the nation to take in an athletic event from anywhere imaginable. And though radio was eventually supplanted by the ubiquity of the television, it continued to thrive, yielding the inaugural all-sport radio station in 1974, New York's City's aptly-named WFAN. Radio played a role in spreading the interest of sports to an entire country, but it also began the relationship between media and advertising, one that continues to flourish to this day.

The invention of the television was a developmental process undertaken by many scientists working independently in various countries and continents from the late 1800s into the end of the 1920s. In the United States, the first commercially produced TV set was manufactured and exhibited by RCA at the 1939 New York World's Fair. Televised broadcasts began shortly thereafter, growing in audience size and interest, so that on July 1, 1941, the Federal Communications Commission (FCC) opened the airwaves to commercial signal transmission, allowing the era of the television to sweep the nation over the remainder of the century. Sports on TV weren't far behind the initial unveiling of the innovation. In fact, a one-camera local broadcast of a 1939 college baseball game between Princeton and Columbia Universities was the first sporting event shown to those lucky enough to own RCA's first sets. That same year, the National Broadcasting

Corporation, or NBC, began putting games and competitions on the air to the residents of New York City. A bicycle race was shown in May 1939, a boxing match held in Yankee Stadium was broadcast in June, the first Major League Baseball (MLB) game was shown on TV in August, and the first professional football game was transmitted on October 22 between the Philadelphia Eagles and the Brooklyn Dodgers (the Dodgers were an NFL team as well as an MLB franchise).

After World War II ended, the television became as ordinary in American homes as the radio had two decades previously. Accordingly, programs including Gillette's *Cavalcade of Sports* made the jump from radio to TV in 1948. By the 1950s, sports was a mainstay of weekend programming, with domestice life expanding to the suburbs and the birth of the nuclear family producing the Baby Boom generation. A television set in the home was as much a necessity as having a dog and two children to go with it.

Without a doubt, the 1950s represented the "Golden Age of Television." Along with scripted mainstays such as *I Love Lucy*, *The Honeymooners*, and *Father Knows Best*, several sports programs emerged as the decade progressed. Examples of these shows include *Sports with Joe Hasel*, *Sportsman's Quiz*, *Fishing and Hunting Club*, *Pro Football Highlights*, Pabst Blue Ribbon's *Bouts*, and Gillette's *Friday Night Fights*. These shows involving athletics created a national dialogue as American citizens discussed the games and contests they witnessed on television, nurturing a closer sense of unity found through the shared experience of knowing that everyone was watching similar events live and directly. Print media picked up steam as well, with the introduction of *Sports Illustrated* in 1954, which had an inaugural cover featuring baseball slugger Eddie Matthews.

As the 1950s ended, technological advances walked hand in hand with the streamlining of television broadcasts. In 1963, audiences were treated to the first use of instant replay for the Army-Navy college football game held on December 7, which, interestingly, was an aspect of TV initially used during the news recap of the murder of Lee Harvey Oswald by Jack Ruby on November 24 of that year. Other features that became commonplace during sports broadcasts included the use of multiple cameras, close-ups on certain players, and slow motion, which greatly popularized the sport of boxing and helped cultivate the legend of Cassius Clay, later known as Muhammad Ali, as one of the most powerful fighters to ever step into a ring.

Other highlights from the 1960s included the creation of ABC's *Wide World of Sports*, hosted by Jim McKay. This show offered U.S. viewers an in-depth look at sports such as Formula 1 car racing, weightlifting, and ski jumping, which were popular in Europe but rarely seen in North America. The show's producer, Roone Arledge, became a pioneer of sports television broadcasting, and his innovations, among them placing multiple microphones on the field and allowing two people to call a game (a play-by-play broadcaster and a color commentator), transformed the landscape of sports forever. *Wide World of Sports* also began the trend of naming the Athlete of the Year, and pushed sports on television into the age of color broadcasting as fan interest in more immersive broadcasts increased. Calling the show a success would be underselling its significance, as it went on a run of thirty-seven consecutive seasons until it was canceled in 1998.

The success of *Wide World of Sports* meant that ABC and Roone Arledge had the bargaining chips available for selling the idea of sports in prime-time programming, and in 1970, the first *Monday Night Football (MNF)* game was broadcast between the New York Jets and the Cleveland Browns on September 21. The show was an instant hit, and *MNF* has been going strong for more than forty years. The 1970s also ushered in cable television, which considerably increased the range of sports being broadcast to American audiences. In 1979, the biggest sports network of all time was founded in Bristol, Connecticut, by Bill Rasmussen and his son Scott. On September 7, 1979, ESPN debuted to cable viewers, and sports fans were treated to the first-ever episode of *SportsCenter*, which seems like it has been airing nonstop ever since. Before long, cable companies nationwide began picking up ESPN, and the network has never looked back, eventually finding a buyer in the Walt Disney Company, which helped its overall worth swell to upwards of $40 billion as it became a bastion for corporate marketing.

Speaking of television revenue growth from sports-based programming, NFL broadcasts brought in a meager $50 million from advertising in 1970, but that number rose to $450 million by 1985. For National Basketball Association (NBA) basketball, the totals jumped like a Michael Jordan dunk, from $2 million to $45 million in that time span. Baseball was no different, with revenue from television broadcasting hitting a grand slam for MLB games, leaping from $18 million to $160 million from 1970 to 1985. It wasn't just network programming on channels such as CBS, NBC, and ABC that brought in large amounts of money. Stations such as WGN and TBS signed large baseball contracts with the Chicago Cubs and Atlanta Braves, respectively, which helped propel team interest into the stratosphere as they were exposed to anyone in the United States with a cable box and a TV set.

It's not hard to believe the growth trends concerning sports and television broadcasting in light of the endless hours of programming that are devoted to athletics in the twenty-first century. It's literally impossible to flip through a channel guide on cable or satellite TV without noticing several sporting events occurring simultaneously on different networks on a twenty-four-hour basis. Television provides fans with a taste of what exists in the world of sports, and that thirst has yet to be fully quenched. With the convergence of various media forms on the Internet, the pervasiveness of sports media is seemingly here to stay and shows no signs of letting up anytime soon. Though there is much competition between networks to reach and maintain audiences, there never seems to be a shortage of new sports programming popping up in new places every year. Who knows how big the reach of sports media can truly be some day?

3

History of the Olympics

T he first Olympic Games took place as a religious festival of athleticism in Olympia, Greece, in the year 776 BCE to commemorate and worship the greatest of all Greek gods, Zeus. The Games were a display of Greek culture and a celebration of art, music, and piety toward the mythological figures who presided over the citizens' hearts and minds. In between athletic competitions, animals were slaughtered to pay penance to Zeus, and the expression of strength and physical prowess played into the Greeks' devoutness and hopefulness for longevity and fertility. These ancient games created a standard off which the modern Olympics are modeled, and in present times, the world gathers once every four years to celebrate sporting achievement and sportsmanship, where integrity and honor take precedent over victory at all costs.

Currently, more than two hundred nations compete in the Winter and Summer Olympics, which are presented at different locations throughout the globe based on a rigorous selection process. Up until 1992, both the Winter and Summer Olympic Games occurred in the same calendar year, but in 1994, the Winter Olympics took place in Lillehammer, Norway, enabling the competitions to be staggered every two years, as they have since that point forward. The first modern Summer Olympics were held in 1896 in Athens, Greece (which has hosted three times in total), and there have been twenty-eight Summer Games in all. The Winter Olympics were launched in 1924 in

Chamonix, France, and the 2014 Olympics in Sochi, Russia, were the twenty-second Winter Games in history.

But let us take a trip back in time to more closely inspect the ancient Olympic Games, which spanned more than 1,100 years, with nearly three hundred official gatherings held in total, until the Roman Empire put an end to the athletic festival under the rule of Emperor Theodosius I in the late fourth century CE. In each of the ancient Olympics, participation was open to all free, male Greek citizens, who would travel to Olympia from the outer reaches of the Athenian Greek Empire. In the corresponding periods of the tournament, the nation's leaders enacted the official decree of an Olympic Truce to ensure safe travel to and from the games. They believed that devoted veneration to Zeus was more important than any petty earthly squabbles that might be going on at the time, so citizens were commanded to temporarily overlook any disputes, quarrels, or all-out wars with other tribes and city-states. Thus, Greek culture was allowed to showcase its athletic glory in a righteous sporting tribute to the gods, something the inhabitants held in the highest of esteem.

According to ancient records, the legend of the Olympics is based on a momentous myth that tells the story of Zeus battling his father, Chronos, for control of the world. They were said to have grappled and fought for several days on the highest mountaintop at Olympia that overlooked the lower southwestern Greek city. In defeating Chronos, Zeus was forever to be considered all-powerful in mind and body, and therefore appropriately praiseworthy. It was in his honor that the people of Greece gathered to compete while incorporating religious ceremonies into the early Olympic celebrations.

The first Olympic Games took place in just one day, but as new events were added to the competition, the festivities covered the course of three days, and then five by the fifth century CE. One of the earliest champions on record was a foot racer known as Astylos of Croton, who came from southern Italy and garnered a total of six olive wreaths, which were used to reward the winner of events as gold medals are today. Incidentally, running was the only sport involved in the first few Olympic Games, with throwing, jumping, wrestling, boxing, and chariot racing being added by the end of the Games' first century. Such growth and expansion should indicate the popularity and importance of the Olympic Games to the people of the Greek Empire in those times, and might help a modern person appreciate that humans have long had the desire to watch and participate in athletic competitions. Though more than two millennia have passed, people still have the same thirst for sports that they did in ancient times.

A great Olympic champion was Leonidas of Rhodes, who competed in various running events, eventually taking home a total of twelve olive wreaths over his time in the Games. Perhaps he can be considered the Michael Phelps of his day. Another champion was known as Melankomas of Caria, who innovated the sport of boxing by winning his fights not by brutally punishing his opponents, but rather by sidestepping opposing punches and staying light on his feet, forever altering the way fighters trained and exercised. The first female champion of the Olympic Games was Cynisca of Sparta, who was bestowed this mark in the history books not because she herself competed, but because she was the owner of the horses that won the chariot race events. In these early times, men were the only individuals allowed to witness and compete in Olympic events, but because Cynisca was a Spartan princess, she was able to breed and train her horses, which were subsequently run in the competitions at Olympia. As owners received the accolades back in the day, Cynisca goes down in history as the first female winner. We will explore the history of women's athletics and media representation in more detail in chapter 6.

As was discussed briefly in chapter 1, the earliest Olympic events were running races, similar to the 200- and 400-meter competitions. The pentathlon was added in 708 BCE and included the javelin throw, the discus toss, a wrestling match, the long jump, and a short foot race. Pankration was brought into the Games in 648 BCE, giving the Olympics the harshest and fiercest sport it had ever seen. This event combined wrestling and boxing with no rules other than prohibiting the gouging out of opponents' eyes. It was a possibility with every match that an athlete might risk death rather than admit defeat. Ancient athletic stadiums were successively built around Greece over the time span of the Olympic Games. In the fourth century CE, the most regal of all stadiums, the Hippodrome of Constantinople, was the crown jewel of sports for the Byzantine Empire, displaying multiple obelisks and hosting some of the greatest horse and chariot races of the era.

It was during the late Roman Empire, around the year 393 CE, that Emperor Theodosius I put a stop to the ancient Olympic Games of Greece. Roman officials claimed that the festivities served only to foster pagan cults and a sense of false glory. Worse, the Greek temples at Olympia were destroyed in 426 CE by Emperor Theodosius II, and the city was sacked and torched to the ground.

Sadly there was no other meaningful, large-scale competition for more than fourteen centuries. Only the images of the ancient Games remained until 1894, when a Frenchman named Pierre de Coubertin helped found the International Olympic Committee, or IOC, as a nonprofit, nongovernmental organization based in Switzerland. Working with the Greek government, Coubertin orchestrated the restoration of the Panathinaiko, or Panathenaic Stadium, in Athens, which served as the marble-etched home of the first modern Olympic Games of 1896. From this point onward, the IOC has always added a dramatic flair to the events, dispensing pomp and pageantry at each Olympics, notably during the opening and closing ceremonies held in the Games' home stadium. These shows rival any Broadway performance, and usually involve the coordination of choreography and audiovisual effects.

With regard to the events, the modern manifestation of the Olympic Games features many different sports unimagined in ancient times. Competitions starting in 1896 included cycling, gymnastics, swimming, shooting, fencing, and weightlifting, as well as classic mainstays such as wrestling, foot racing, boxing, javelin, and discus. As of the 2012 Games, there was a total of 302 different events in twenty-six sports, including several eclectic choices such as judo, table tennis, handball, tae kwon do, and water polo.

Not surprisingly, given the leadership of de Coubertin, the 1900 Summer Olympic Games took place in Paris, France, as did the 1924 Summer Olympics. But it wasn't until that same year, 1924, that the first Winter Games occurred, taking place in the French village of Chamonix. These games were overseen by de Coubertin, who pushed for a type of competition for those involved in alpine sports in higher-altitude regions as well as those from colder climates, such as the Scandinavian sections of northern Europe.

The 1924 Winter Olympics featured twelve events, including such sports as figure skating, ice hockey, curling, bobsledding, and the biathlon, a mixture of target shooting and cross-country skiing that is still an Olympic favorite. This sports jamboree was initially billed as the "International Winter Sports Week" and included sixteen nations with three hundred athletes in total, thirteen of whom were female. The Norwegians won the most medals that year, taking home a total of seventeen prizes, while the United States came in fifth in team rankings, with four overall medals. By the next Games of 1928, held in St. Moritz, Switzerland, the international sports competition acquired its current signature of the Winter Olympics, and the race was on for king of the mountain—literally speaking for the downhill skiing competition, at least.

The United States' first opportunity to host the Winter Olympics came in 1932, when the Games took place in Lake Placid, New York, a venue that also hosted in 1980. The 1960 Winter Olympics were held in Squaw Valley, California (a mountain range that lies in the Lake Tahoe area of the Sierra Nevada), and in 2002, Salt Lake City, Utah, hosted the Games that saw seventy-seven nations vying for medals in seventy-eight events (with Norway taking the most gold medals once again).

One of the primary virtues promoted by the IOC is its insistence that the Games take place in a harmonious environment of sportsmanship and integrity. Political statements are shunned, and the athletes themselves are expected to behave courteously and with honor. An excerpt of the Olympic Oath, which is read before every Games by a representative athlete and a judge on behalf of all participants, follows as such: *"In the name of all the competitors, I promise that we shall take part in these Olympic Games respecting and abiding the rules which govern them…in the true spirit of sportsmanship, for the glory of sport and the honor of our teams."*

Nonetheless, the modern Olympic Games were not without their share of controversy throughout the twentieth century. First off, there was the 1936 Summer Olympics held in Berlin, Germany, which was under the rule of the Nazi Party and Führer Adolf Hitler at the time. The bid for the games was actually awarded in 1931, two years prior to Nazi rule, and it is clear that the world could not have seen the devastating future on the horizon with Hitler's Germany. Although the Nazis sought to promote their agenda of racial supremacy and the Aryan man as the prototypical human specimen, the United States' Jesse Owens, an African American track & field star, took home four gold medals under the watchful eye of Hitler, who was present at most of the proceedings. Earlier that year, Germany also hosted the Winter Olympic Games, the last time one country was able to put on both games in the same calendar term. That too was marked by Nazi propaganda and iconographic symbolism.

As the twentieth century progressed, the Olympics were marred by global unrest on several occasions. The 1940 and 1944 Olympic Games were called off because of World War II. In 1976, many African nations boycotted the Summer Games held in Montreal, Canada, because the IOC would not ban New Zealand from competition; its rugby squad had played games in Apartheid-era South Africa. In 1980, Cold War tensions led the United States and sixty-four other nations to boycott the Summer Olympics in Moscow in response to the Russian invasion of Afghanistan in 1979. As a counter-move to these actions, the Soviet Union and its communist allies boycotted the 1984 Summer Games held in Los Angeles, a decision that enabled the United States to take home a record eighty-three gold medals, the most for any one nation in any single Olympics (a record that is most deserving of a very large asterisk).

With the fall of the Iron Curtain in the early 1990s and the banishment of South African apartheid in 1993, global tensions have eased to the point where the Games have included more than two hundred nations as of the 2012 London Summer Olympics. Sadly, though, the Olympics also have had their share of violent tragedies, including the murder of five Israeli athletes and six coaches in the Olympic Village by Palestinian assassins during the 1972 Summer Games held in Munich, Germany, as well as a bombing at the Centennial Olympic Park during the 1996 Summer Games held in Atlanta, Georgia. The Olympics, as humans do, have always found a way to move past misfortunes, and in August 2016, the country of Brazil will host the first-ever South American–based Games in the city of Rio de Janeiro.

Media coverage of the Olympic Games has grown by leaps and bounds over the past one hundred years with the advent of the convergent technical innovations available in the twenty-first century. The 1908 Olympics in London featured newspaper reporting, photos for the first time ever, and even a few reels of film to be shown in silent movie theaters around the globe. The 1924 Paris Olympics introduced live radio broadcasting to the Games, enabling a newfound immersion possible for European sports fans, especially for those in London listening to the BBC. In 1936, at the Summer Olympics held in Berlin, Germany, closed-circuit TV was used for the first time, piping feeds out to cinemas throughout the city, thus creating the world's first sports bars. London's 1948 Summer Games introduced public television broadcasting of the events, ushering in the first-ever TV payment rights, which were funded by the BBC. Satellite television debuted in the summer of 1960, with feeds beamed from Rome to the United States at a cost of $3.9 million, covered by CBS, to bring the competition to American TV sets live and direct. Finally, concerning the Olympics' existence online, the 2000 Summer Games hosted by Sydney, Australia, introduced the first Olympic Internet contract, which was signed by NBC in the United States for $715 million, allowing the network to stream events over cyberspace. For the 2008 Beijing Summer Olympics, mobile smartphone application technology began sending packets of data around the globe for the first time in history, with social networking sites such as Facebook and Twitter enabling billions of people to connect and interact directly worldwide, giving live updates and opinions throughout the Games.

Some of the United States' greatest Olympic moments involve such names as Jesse Owens (four track & field gold medals in 1936), Mark Spitz (seven gold medals in swimming in 1972), Wilma Rudolph (three sprinting golds in 1960), Michael Phelps (a record eighteen swimming gold medals across three games from 2004 to 2012), and the 1980 American ice hockey team, who defeated a powerhouse Soviet Union squad in a miraculous upset in Lake Placid, New York, en route to a gold medal. A list of Olympic heroes could go on and on, and the beauty of the Games is that each one gives athletes from every nation on earth a chance to represent their citizens, playing and competing with pride in hope of becoming an idol who will be revered by fans for centuries to come. This, ultimately, was the motivation to hold the Olympics in the first place.

The Paralympic Games, or Paralympics, were started in 1948 by a German neurologist, Dr. Ludwig Guttmann, and were initially known as the International Wheelchair Games, held in the town of Stoke Mandeville, England. They began as a forum for British war veterans who had suffered debilitating injuries during World War II and wished to show they were still capable of competing in a way that displayed the spirit of organized athletics. Dr. Guttmann wanted to illustrate that sports competitions for people with disabilities would be equivalent to those of the Olympic Games, and the events were an immediate success for all those involved.

By 1960, the first official Paralympic Games were held in Rome, coinciding with the Summer Olympics taking place in the city, and the competition was no longer exclusively for wounded war veterans. In those inaugural Games of 1960, four hundred athletes participated in twenty-three events, and the Paralympics have continued since. Though the first four Paralympics were open only to those in wheelchairs, the 1976 Games extended the definition of disabilities to allow more than 1,600 athletes from forty different nations to partake in the events. That same year, the initial Winter Paralympic Games were brought into existence in a town known as Örnsköldsvik, Sweden, with 198 athletes competing in Alpine and Nordic skiing. As of the 2012 Summer Paralympics, the Games involved more than 4,300 athletes from 164 nations.

The current Paralympic Games include any disabled athletes with amputations, blindness, cerebral palsy, or any other mobility disorder. The events take place in the same calendar years as the Winter and Summer Olympics, commencing immediately after the end of those Games. The Paralympics are governed by the International Paralympic Committee, or IPC, which is based in Bonn, Germany, and has 174 different national members who have their own Paralympic Committees.

As this chapter has illustrated, both ancient and modern human beings alike have shared the desire to compete against one another in official athletic events to display physical proficiency and adept skill in specific sports. The original ancient Olympics held in Greece in 776 BCE may not have looked exactly the same as the modern Games taking place in the twenty-first century, but there is little doubt that a casual observer in either era would know precisely what she or he was witnessing, no matter the time or place. Organized sporting events give people a chance to practice and become specialists in their areas of expertise in hopes of demonstrating to the world just how great of a champion each and every one of them can be. Children see the heroes of the Olympics and dream about becoming one someday, providing the motivation to propel humans toward a representative greatness that will inspire societies to push farther and faster, in a manner that involves honor and integrity every step of the way.

4

International Sports

The history of sports involves thousands of years of progress and embraces every area of the Earth. From a local perspective, sports seem indelibly American, but in reality, athletic competition is vastly more international than most people imagine. Each society uses sports in some fashion as a representation of skill and physical prowess, so this chapter will accordingly investigate sports on a global level. Specifically, it will examine the inception, expansion, and current incarnations of athletics around the world.

With an estimated three billion sports fans worldwide, it seems logical to begin a book chapter on international sports by discussing the most popular one on the planet, as well as one of the oldest in existence. It is a simple game that uses a soft or rubberized ball kicked between teammates without the use of the hands in hopes of advancing into the opponent's side of the field. The object is to score a goal by kicking or heading the ball into a goaltended net. Yes, the game of soccer, or football as the rest of the world refers to it, has been around in some form or another since 206 B.C.E., when the Chinese used the sport of tsu chu, or cuju, as an athletic exercise to sharpen the skills of those involved in military training. Several hundred years later, around 644 CE, the Japanese began exhibiting athletic dexterity in a game known as kemari. However, this foot and ball combination was more of a noncompetitive sport resembling hacky sack, with players standing in a circle and passing a grain-stuffed ball to one another in the air with adept skill and accuracy.

One of the cultures most commonly associated with soccer is that of the British, mainly because of the billion-dollar English Premier League, which features the world's greatest players year after year. However, the origins of football in Europe date back to around the eighth century, specifically taking place in the British Isles and resembling a combination of rugby and Gaelic football. This primitive manifestation usually consisted of contests between neighboring villages, but the structure of the game required some fine-tuning before becoming the modern version of soccer that fans enjoy today. There were even versions of the game known as "mob football," wherein the number of players on each side was limitless and the rules were sparse, if they existed at all.

Some historians note the symbolic nature of an early version of football, with the ball itself representing the sun, which needed to be kicked and conquered to ensure a bountiful harvest. Others point to pagan customs involving fertility rights and emblematic proceeds in the eyes of the gods as motivations for wanting to "win" the competition. No matter what the case, there has always been some positive incentive associated with victory, and this element of sports and athletics overall can surely be appreciated by any current-day sports fan.

Several important periods associated with the development of soccer include the year 1314, when the lord mayor of London declared an end to all football played in the city because of the chaos surrounding the game. Anyone caught competing would be prosecuted and imprisoned immediately. These prohibitions continued throughout the next 150 years under the rules of King Edward III, King Richard II, King Henry IV, and King Henry V, who all claimed that the game of football prevented men from achieving the proper military training necessary to protect the nation, especially archery. King James I of Scotland even issued a proclamation in 1424 that was backed by the Scottish parliament stating that "na man play at the fute-ball!" For some reason, this decree didn't hold anyone back in the least, as the sport began to flourish and move into neighboring countries.

Soccer finally found stable footing in Elizabethan times, when England was under the rule of Queen Elizabeth I from 1558 to 1603. At the same time on the continent, the Italian Renaissance ushered in an intense popularity for the game that was previously unseen in civil societies. In Italy, a version of football went by the name of calcio fiorentino (roughly meaning "Florentine Kick"), which was a more organized version of the English variation. However, it still resembled rugby in that players could hold and carry the ball in their arms. In this form, calcio players wore different colored uniforms to represent their side, and the game was played in enclosed areas, usually in soft pits of sand to cushion harsh tackles to the ground.

In Britain, football still remained suppressed, if not outright banned in most places until the nineteenth century, when schools began developing styles of the game for each area of the country. Space limitations generally determined how matches were staged, and players' skill sets had to adjust to competing on makeshift fields such as walled-in blacktop playgrounds. Overall, it was in these times that the sport was deemed a benefit to society, specifically encouraging honorable human qualities such as loyalty, sportsmanship, selflessness, and coordination, as well as cooperation and team unity.

In 1846, Dr. Thomas Arnold penned the first official rules for the game of rugby, which emphasized the handling and carrying of the ball while outlawing the use of the foot to kick the ball. It is this, perhaps, that propelled the creation of an official delineated form of football for those who felt that this foot-only variety of the sport was the most dexterous and challenging representation of athletic expertise. Accordingly, in 1863 at Cambridge University, a group of players felt that Dr. Arnold's rugby rules put too much emphasis on the use of the hands and arms to transport the ball while at the same time being too lenient regarding the kicking of legs and shins to disrupt opposing players. Consequently, they established a group of clubs to play the game of football that they envisioned as most proper, and on October 26, 1863, eleven schools sent representatives to a place called Freemason's Tavern to discuss the formation of a set of rules for the sport of football. It marked the birth of the Football Association, also known as the FA, which became official on December 8 of that year. This sporting body signaled the divergence of soccer and rugby forever, and explicitly labeled football as a game of skill and coordination whereby a player was prohibited from using his or her hands during the game to advance or maneuver the ball at any time. The rest, as they say, is most certainly history.

Three years after the creation of the Football Association, the game's ninety-minute duration was established as the most ideal length for each match. Several years after that, a standard-size ball was recognized to ensure uniform play within the league. By 1871, the FA had fifty clubs, and the association's first knockout tournament, called the FA Cup, was held in 1872, with a team called the Wanderers taking the first title. In November of that same year, football saw its first-ever international matchup, with England competing against neighboring Scotland in an official game that ended in a 0-0 tie. In 1873, Scotland formed its own version of the Football Association, while Wales developed a national FA in 1875, as did Ireland in 1880.

The influence of these football organizations in Britain soon spread the game to all areas of the globe. Netherlands and Denmark established football leagues in 1889, New Zealand in 1891, Argentina in 1893, and Chile in 1895, along with Switzerland and Belgium that same year. Italy's first soccer league started in 1889, and Germany and Uruguay founded theirs in 1900, while Hungary began a league in 1901, with Finland finding football fever in 1907.

Most important of all things football-related, the international governing body known as FIFA was established in May of 1904. The Fédération Internationale de Football Association kicked off in Paris, France. It is now a billion-dollar entity with headquarters in Zurich, Switzerland. By 1912, twenty-one different nations were members of the organization, with that number swelling to forty countries by the year 1930, when the inaugural FIFA World Cup was held in Uruguay. The host nation was crowned World Cup champions in a 4-2 victory over Argentina, and for Uruguay, it was a successful defense of their 1928 gold medal from the Summer Olympics held in Amsterdam, Netherlands. Since this opening FIFA World Cup, there has been a tournament every four years, except for the World War II–era years 1942 and 1946. FIFA is currently comprised of 208 official nations who compete in the build-up between World Cups to acquire the coveted spots on the world stage, of which there are only thirty-two.

This game that most of the world calls "football" is known as soccer in the United States, through an interesting turn of language. Early twentieth-century Americans began using term "football" in 1913 with the creation of the United States Football Association, now known as the United States Soccer Federation. However, there was some confusion because a quite different game of football was already being played in America. Out of the name United Stated Football Association, referring to the game played with a round ball and no use of hands came the emphasis on "association," that morphed into "soccer." For sticklers of the sport's title, the most particular way to refer to it would be to call it "association football," but many could live and die without hearing that phrase as denoting a soccer match occurring anywhere specific.

U.S. soccer truly began in 1894 with the American League of Professional Football Clubs, which was started by the National League of Professional Baseball Clubs (known presently as MLB's National League) in order to fill stadiums with sporting events during off-season months. The game became popular in metropolitan areas such as New York, Chicago, and Pittsburgh, and in 1904 the entire U.S. Olympic soccer team was comprised of players from St. Louis. Upon a FIFA request in 1912, the U.S. Football Association was founded in 1913 after merging with the American Amateur Football Association. After World War I ended in 1921, U.S. soccer attempted its first official league, knows as the American Soccer League (ASL), which lasted for twelve years until 1933 when it disbanded because of the Great Depression. The league rose from the ashes, though, and existed in one form or another in the United States until 1983.

Perhaps the most intriguing version of American soccer existed from 1978 to 1992 as a turf-based sport known as the Major Indoor Soccer League. This type of soccer allowed players to bounce the ball off walls to pass to themselves, and featured international Brazilian superstar Pelé, who played for the New York Cosmos. The Cosmos were also a part of the North American Soccer League, or NASL, which played matches from 1968 to 1984 throughout the United States and Canada. This league also featured indoor games in the late 1970s and early 1980s.

The great leap forward for soccer in America came as the United States hosted the 1994 FIFA World Cup, which was played in cities such as Los Angeles, Chicago, Orlando, Detroit, Washington, D.C., and Dallas. The U.S. soccer team found success with a win over Colombia, but eventually lost to runner-up Brazil in the first round of the knockout stage in a game held on July 4.

Fan interest in American soccer soared right after the tournament, and Major League Soccer, or MLS, began play in 1996 with ten original teams. The league continues to this day and features players who have come from and gone on to bigger and better leagues in Europe. Famed English football standout David Beckham made his debut for the MLS's L.A. Galaxy as a "designated player" in 2007, and this type of personnel allocation has allowed aging stars such as France's Thierry Henry to play in the United States as his career came to a close. Surely, the MLS will look to expand in fan awareness and worldwide prominence as the years go by, but the true test of American soccer will be determined by future showings at the FIFA World Cup. Winning on the world stage is the one indisputable way to engender a lasting bond between fans and a sporting team, and to this day, the United States has yet to prove it belongs in the upper echelon of great footballing nations. All it would take would be one World Cup win to achieve this status, so this hope for greatness will always exist.

The other hugely popular North American sport that also has an immense following in European countries such as Sweden, Finland, and the Czech Republic is the cold-weather competition known as ice hockey. Played with stick in hand, hockey is much like soccer in that the ultimate goal is to move the puck into the opponent's zone in order to shoot the flat, frozen, rubber object into a small net minded by a padded goaltender. At any time, a hockey team is allowed six players per side, one of whom is most always the goalie (save for desperate times in one-goal deficit situations). The game is divided up into three separate periods with an intermission in between each session of play.

The history of hockey in a non-ice form dates back several thousand years based on various historical records around Ireland, but the most closely related version can be traced to the sport of field hockey, which was played in England in the seventeenth and eighteenth centuries by villagers looking to prove their fierceness, pride, and durability. In these matches, teams would sometimes consist of more than one hundred players apiece, with few rules to inhibit grievous injuries or dangerous maneuvers. Because of the chaotic nature of these competitions, the Eton College of England drafted rules in the mid-1800s to restore some sanity to the game; then, in 1886, an official Hockey Association was formed at Trinity College of Cambridge, England, to write some uniform guidelines for its seven London clubs, as well as how to implement them by match referees. With newfound authority, umpires could now referee and regulate games, finally allowing rival spectators to enjoy an organized form of a sport the masses soon came to love.

Elsewhere, ice sports were played in Northern Europe, where a stick-and-ball game of ice golf existed as early as the seventeenth-century in the Netherlands. It wasn't until the end of the 1800s that John George Creighton laid down the original rules of ice hockey in his hometown of Montreal, Quebec, Canada. Now considered to be the Father of Ice Hockey, Creighton's creation first appeared at McGill University in March 1875. Two nine-man squads squared off in a game witnessed by student onlookers as well as several people from the local Montreal newspaper. The rules were officially penned by a group of hockey enthusiasts at McGill University in 1879, establishing the goal mouth as six feet wide and the game duration as sixty minutes—both of which are still in use in modern hockey leagues such as the NHL.

In terms of organized ice hockey, the sport took no time at all to capture the hearts and minds of the Canadian public. By 1883, less than ten years after the game's invention, the McGill University club took the first-ever national championship known as the Carnival Cup played at Montreal's Winter Carnival. To this day, Canadians look to Montreal as the revered birthplace of their beloved national pastime (even though lacrosse is officially Canada's national game). During the following decade, dozens of amateur leagues debuted around Canada, and by the 1890s it was clear that an overall organization of the various teams would be necessary. Thanks to the stewardship of the sixteenth Earl of Derby, Canada's Governor General Frederick Arthur Stanley, a competition was structured wherein the victors would receive Lord Stanley's prized silver teapot, soon to be known as the Stanley Cup. The Montreal Hockey Club won the first one at the Dominion Hockey Challenge of 1893, and teams continued to fight, literally most times, for the trophy on a yearly basis from this point forward.

By the early 1900s, hockey fever had swept Canada, and the sport was being played in many different locations across England and Northern Europe. Some believe its popularity had much to do with the establishment of the first-ever Winter Olympics, which took place shortly after the end of World War I in 1924 in Chamonix, France. Not coincidently, the Canadian national team took home the gold medal, outscoring teams in the group stage by a composite total of 110 to 3 over just four games.

In Canada, interest in playing ice hockey kept swelling, and in the 1910s a league known as the National Hockey Association, or NHA, was formed in Montreal. The creators of the NHA established more rules for the game, giving the competition its modern feel and dividing play into three twenty-minute periods. By 1917, the organization's name was changed to the National Hockey League, or NHL, and four original teams skated toe-to-toe to play for the Stanley Cup—two from Montreal, one from Ottawa, and one from Toronto. In 1924, the Boston Bruins became the first American team in the NHL, and by 1942, the "Original Six"—Boston, Chicago, Detroit, Montreal, Toronto, and New York—became the NHL's identity for the next twenty-five years until expansion opened the league to more team memberships in 1967.

Currently, thirty different teams compete in the NHL each season, most of them based in the United States. The annual revenue of the NHL is more than $2.25 billion, a high figure, but this pales in comparison with the revenue of leagues such as the MLB ($7.5 billion), NBA ($4 billion), and NFL (a whopping $9.5 billion in revenue annually). Nonetheless, hockey is still the backbone of

Canadian sporting culture and the paradigm of rugged durability and tenacious determination, as well as honorable sportsmanship.

Moving on, a peculiar sport to many Americans is known as Australian Rules Football. The game is a combination of football and rugby that has been played Down Under since 1859, when Tom Wills came home from a trip to England and formed the Melbourne Football Club. A true pioneer for the sport of Australian Rules Football, Wills worked with another Australian, Henry Harrison, to create the first laws of Australian Rules Football. The rules called for an oval ball instead of a round one, and made use of the drop kick as one of the more unusual ways for a player to score additional points.

In the gameplay of modern Australian Rules Football, opposing sides compete on an elliptical field that measures 150 meters long and 135 meters wide, much larger than an American football field. Teams are made up of 18 eighteen players per side. Although competitors can roam freely from end to end like those in soccer (such as when a defenseman scores a goal on a corner kick), there are both designated offensive and defensive positions, as well as "ruckmen," who patrol the center of the field to facilitate possession of the ball for their side.

The official length of time for an Australian Rules Football match is eighty minutes, plus additional time-on if necessary, separated into four twenty-minute quarters. A game is won by the team that scores the most points. Scoring comes by kicking the ball between the highest (and two most center of the four total) upright goal posts, yielding six points, or by sending a kick ball between one of the inner posts and one of the two outward and lower posts, which awards the team one point. A single point can also be scored if the ball is transported across the goal line while being possessed. The main object of the game, though, is to have a player catch a kicked pass that has traveled more than 15 fifteen meters, which is known as a "mark"—a representation of supreme and valued athletic prowess. Accomplishing a mark allows the catching player a free drop kick from the location at which he caught the ball, and the aim is to accurately strike the ball in between the center posts for a six-point goal.

The sport's top alliance is known as the Australian Football League, or AFL, which has been in existence since 1897, although it was named the Victorian Football League up until 1996. There are eighteen teams competing in the AFL, with the squad from Melbourne, called Essendon, holding the most champion-ships in league history. In 2013, the revenue for the Australian Football League was $425 million, which should give some perspective when comparing it to the NHL or the other big three American sports of football, baseball, and basketball. Like any other business entity, the AFL has corporate sponsors, and the teams themselves as well as the stadiums all have found some financial companionship from big business.

The final international sport examined in this chapter is a variation of baseball that has been around far longer than America's pastime. Originally played during the Renaissance around the year 1550 in Northern Europe, cricket was officially enshrined in writing in 1697 in a "great match" played in Sussex, England, which was documented by a local newspaper, the *Foreign Post*. Growing in prominence over the next hundred years, cricket was spread across the globe because of the enormous reach of the British Empire, bringing the game to countries such as India, Sri Lanka, New Zealand, Australia, and Kenya.

Cricket is still immensely popular to this day, and there is a multitude of teams and leagues that compete worldwide, all following the same basic rules. Cricket squads have eleven players on each side, playing on a round field, where a bowler essentially pitches a hard ball overhead that bounces towards a batter armed with a cricket bat, standing at attention, ready to swing underhanded. As in baseball, runs are accumulated via quality hits by the batter, and games are comprised of various amounts of innings depending on the predetermined structure of the match. A batter is "dismissed," or called out and unable to continue, once a bowler has bounced the hard ball past his swing and taken out one of the wickets staked into the ground behind the batter.

The current most popular variation of cricket is called Twenty20, which is a shortened version of the game that usually lasts about three hours from start to finish. In another style of the sport, cricket "tests" are played as a series of matches over several days, lasting for five days in modern times. To give an idea of the vast adoration some countries have for the sport of cricket, it is said that of the ten most popular sports in India, cricket is nine of them. This joke should give an indication of how some tastes that are distinctly international might be strange to American sports enthusiasts, but such a fact does not make these sports any less relevant or of any minor cultural significance to those in the nations who routinely play them on a daily basis.

5

Racial Barriers

R ace is a social construct. This means that one set of people, usually those with the most power, decides what advantage their group has over another. Race is based on physical characteristics, often the color of skin, but ethnic differences can be much more subtle while no less significant. It is illegal to discriminate on the basis of race in the United States, though for a vast number of years, the exact opposite was the case. An unfortunate aspect of organized athletics is the lack of inclusion for many different types of people, whether the segregations are based on gender, sexual orientation, or, in the case of this chapter's central focus, racial and ethnic discrimination. As was discussed in the previous chapter, women were barred from participating in or even watching the ancient Olympic Games held in Greece, and to this day, some cultures prohibit females from sitting in the stands at sporting events.

The barriers of inequality have been a constant in America, a deeply regrettable and unjust result of the slave trade from Africa. Even the Emancipation Proclamation by Abraham Lincoln in 1863 and the subsequent end of the Civil War did little to change the lives of African Americans, for a post-slavery United States relegated the freed slaves and their descendants to the status of second-class citizens in much of the country. Indeed, the history of America is marred by the past indiscretions of the ruling class over African Americans, fostering an environment of discrimination that can still be found today.

While a disproportionately high number of African American athletes in some of the highest-grossing professional sports in the United States does exist, such as in NBA basketball and NFL football, there remains an equally lopsided balance of white head coaches, owners, and general managers in those leagues. This chapter will serve to explore the various barriers of the last one-hundred-plus years in organized American athletics, detailing the men and women who have stood out and stepped forward as trailblazers for African Americans everywhere, allowing small strides to be made along the way to open doors to new opportunities for future athletes. Let us first begin by looking at the era of the United States after the Civil War, specifically at the end of the nineteenth century.

An important African American in the history of sports is a relatively unknown man, William Henry Lewis, who was born in 1868 in Berkley, Virginia. The son of former slaves, Lewis was precocious in his youth, enrolling at the all-black Virginia Normal and Collegiate Institute at the young age of fifteen. Through assistance from the president of that school, Lewis was able to join Amherst College when he turned eighteen, where he not only excelled at public speaking, but also developed a leadership role on the 1888 Amherst football squad, making it the first racially integrated sports team in the history of America.

By 1891, Lewis served as team captain at Amherst, where he excelled not only in athletics, but also in academics. In 1892 he gained admission to Harvard Law School, where he flourished athletically, playing the position of center for the Crimson football team that dominated the era, earning All-American honors each of the two seasons he played, making himself the first African American to be given that honor. On top of it all, Lewis served as team captain to finish the 1893 season, and then went on to coach the team to a combined 114-15-5 win-loss record over ten seasons until 1906. In that time span, Lewis penned an instructional manual on football while simultaneously serving as a state legislator. In 1910, President William Howard Taft bestowed one of the highest honors upon Lewis, naming him Assistant Attorney General of the United States, another first for an African American.

Despite his athletic greatness and political success, Lewis still faced racial discrimination from many whites in the northern states; fellow lawyers forced him out of the American Bar Association (ABA) in 1911. Notwithstanding his loss of membership from the ABA, Lewis was still able to thrive as a private practice lawyer and worked diligently for civil rights over the course of his life, cementing his legacy as a groundbreaking African American hero. William H. Lewis' contributions to society will be remembered forever, thanks in part to his induction into the College Football Hall of Fame in 2009.

A man who became one of the greatest boxing champions in history went by the plain but memorable name of Jack Johnson. Born in 1878 in Galveston, Texas, Johnson was a man of brute strength with a devastating uppercut, but he was a fluid fighter who used his intellect to patiently frustrate his opponents in matches that lasted up to twenty rounds. His professional career began inauspiciously at age nineteen with a loss to a middleweight fighter in his hometown in Texas. Johnson soon grew stronger and tougher, especially after serving several days in jail for participating in an illegal bout in February 1901. By 1903, he was fighting as a heavyweight and was able to win the World Colored Heavyweight Championship over a man named Denver Ed Childs.

Finally, in 1908, after years of pleading for a chance to compete for the universal boxing title, Jack Johnson fought and defeated Tommy Burns, the Canadian crusher who held the World Heavyweight Championship crown. The bout took place in Sydney, Australia, on December 26, otherwise known as Boxing Day (so named in the British Empire for the boxed presents people would receive from their employers the day after Christmas; this name was also quite appropriate for the day of a title fight). Johnson's victory made him the first African American heavyweight champion ever, setting off race riots across the United States. Johnson's will was unsettling for many whites, and a plea rose from bigoted sports fans to either rule him ineligible or have some "Great White Hope" step forward to defeat the rightful title holder. Johnson refused to back down and was able to hold his title for years, even defeating former champion James Jeffries in Reno, Nevada, in 1910 in a match dubbed the first "Fight of the Century." It wasn't until April 1915, when Johnson was conquered by an ex-cowboy from Kansas named Jess Willard, that he relinquished his championship belt, finishing off an epic reign that lasted nearly seven years. Several fights, including the 1910 match against Jeffries, were captured on film and are now part of the National Film Registry. Truly, Jack Johnson deserves to be in any conversation concerning the greatest boxers of all time.

Another legendary fighter who will always be mentioned with the greats of boxing is Joe Louis (full name Joseph Louis Barrow), an African American heavyweight who held the championship for an astounding eleven years and eight months, from 1937 to 1949, successfully defending his title twenty-five times. Nicknamed the Brown Bomber, Louis was born in Lafayette, Alabama, in 1914 but moved to Detroit, Michigan, in 1926, when his family traveled north in the Great Migration. Louis found it very difficult to get any opportunities as a black man to challenge for the heavyweight crown in the 1930s, despite his unbeaten record in local professional fights—a residue of the racial abuse Jack Johnson had endured. Louis' celebrity began to rise in 1935 after a sixth-round knockout of former world heavyweight champion Primo Carnera. In 1937, despite having suffered a loss to Third Reich fighter Max Schmeling in 1936, he was finally given a shot at the title in a bout against James J. Braddock. Braddock knocked Louis down in the sixth round, but the Brown Bomber rose to his feet and won the championship via an eighth-round knockout in front of forty-five thousand fans at Chicago's Comiskey Park. In a rematch, Louis defeated Schmeling for the title defense in 1938. Prior to the fight, President Franklin Roosevelt called Louis to encourage him, and to let him know how important this match against the Nazi's prized Schmeling was. After topping Schmeling, Louis became an unstoppable force in the ring for the next decade, rising to mythical status and the face of American sporting power throughout the 1940s. Joe Louis is known around the world as one of the greatest sports heroes of any race, but more importantly, as a man who transcended athletics and became an American emblem of the twentieth century. His greatness will never be diminished or forgotten.

There were other athletes who made major contributions to the recognition of African Americans as athletic champions as well. One of them was Frederick "Fritz" Pollard. Born in Chicago in 1894, Pollard played football at Brown University in Providence, Rhode Island, helping the team reach the Rose Bowl in 1916 as a running back, thus becoming the first African American to play in the heralded game. Directly following his college graduation, he became a football coach at Lincoln University in Pennsylvania, and then head coach of various semiprofessional football teams over the next two years. Finally, in 1920, Pollard and a man named Bobby Marshall became the first two African Americans to play in the National Football League (NFL), with Pollard making his debut for the Akron Pros, serving as a coach as well. In 1922, Pollard joined the Milwaukee Badgers of the NFL, and that team shortly thereafter became known for its inclusion of several African American players. Pollard's place in history was secure, and in 2005, he was inducted into the National Football League Hall of Fame.

In the time of the Great Depression during the 1930s, one African American athlete stands out from the rest as perhaps the greatest sportsman of all. Jesse Owens was mentioned briefly in chapter 3, but his importance as a legend is worth noting in more detail here, especially for his performance in the 1936 Summer Olympics held in Berlin, Germany, before Nazi leader Adolph Hitler. Born in September 1913 in the small, Southern town of Oakville, Alabama, Owens grew up in Cleveland, Ohio, after his family moved there in 1922. In Ohio, Owens tied the world record in the 100-yard dash as a nineteen-year-old high school student, eventually going on to become a track star at Ohio State University. At Ohio State, Owens set a record for most individual National Collegiate Athletic Association (NCAA) track & field championships, amassing four titles each in the years 1935 and 1936 and setting or tying three world records. Not just a sprinter, Owens was above and beyond the competition, literally, setting records in the long jump and in the low hurdles race in the collegiate national championship meet of 1936.

Indeed, 1936 would be the Year of Jesse Owens. His talents as an overall athlete were put on full display at the Summer Olympics in Berlin, which occurred under the watchful eye of Hitler, who attended many of the events. The Nazi Party had hoped the Games would solidify their assertion that the Aryan Race was superior to all, but Owens put a quick end to that, dashing to gold medals in the 100-meter, 200-meter, and 4x100-meter races, while also taking home a fourth gold in the long jump.Hitler refused to congratulate anyone in person following Owens' victories. Upon returning to the United States, Jesse Owens was treated to a ticker tape parade in New York City. He stands as a marker for outstanding achievements in Olympic athletics and American sports overall. Owens was quite literally and figuratively an All-American hero.

Sadly, the plight of African Americans as second-class citizens still tarnished the reputation of the United States after World War II, and this type of discrimination was best illustrated by the Negro leagues of baseball that existed from the 1920s to 1951. The leagues were formed because blacks were not allowed to play for Major League Baseball teams. Though there was never an official decree on the part of the MLB to formally exclude blacks and Latinos from becoming paid athletes, no franchise had anyone besides white players on their Major League rosters or in their minor league farm systems.

Everything changed in 1946. That year, a fast and powerful phenom named Jack Roosevelt "Jackie" Robinson signed a contract with the Brooklyn Dodgers of the MLB, making him the first African American to break the color barrier in the sport. Jackie Robinson's talents were so complete that he was placed on the team's opening-day roster, making history in a game on April 15, 1947, that saw him start at first base and bat second in the order, scoring one run in the game.

But Robinson's ascent to the Major Leagues was far from direct and not without its bumps along the way. Like most American men of that decade, Robinson was drafted into the United States Army in 1942, where he served as a second lieutenant in a tank battalion in Fort Hood, Texas. While in the Army, Robinson faced racial bias like any other African American at the time, but he never wavered under bigotry and stood up for himself at all times, even during a dispute on a bus that left him charged with insubordination and other character-smearing falsehoods. Thankfully, the resulting judicial action kept him from deploying to Europe to fight in the war. After an acquittal in his court martial trial and an honorable discharge from the military, Robinson was relegated to the Negro leagues, playing ball for the Kansas City Monarchs in the year 1945, hitting for a high average and stealing bases with his blazing speed. There, Major League scouts marveled at his aptitude as a ballplayer, and the Dodgers eventually signed Robinson, in part because of his calm demeanor and willingness to play with honor while not responding to the inevitable racial epithets that were sure to come his way.

Robinson had a stellar career in Brooklyn, helping his team capture the 1955 World Series before becoming the first African American elected to the Baseball Hall of Fame in 1962. After his playing career was over, Robinson maintained a high-profile public persona, becoming the first black vice president of an American corporation, all the time speaking on behalf of African Americans and the need for more civil rights for all. He served on the board of the National Association for the Advancement of Colored People (NAACP) until 1967. The number 42 is synonymous with Jackie Robinson, and Major League Baseball has bestowed the honor of retiring that number for all thirty of its teams. Plaques with the number and Robinson's name are displayed in every Major League ballpark in the United States.

Two revolutionary African American female athletes who came to prominence shortly after Jackie Robinson are Althea Gibson and Wilma Rudolph, who competed in international tennis and track & field, respectively. We will discuss both women in further detail in the next chapter, but Gibson was the first African American to compete in worldwide professional tennis events. She captured multiple championships in the sport, including the 1956 French Open (her first major title), as well as Wimbledon in 1957 along with two other Grand Slams that year. Wilma Rudolph was easily the fastest woman in the world throughout the 1950s and early 1960s. Rudolph was the first African American woman to earn three Olympic gold medals, which she did at the 1960 Summer Olympics held in Rome, Italy (high jumper Alice Coachman had been the first female African American gold medalist in the 1948 London Olympics). Each woman performed with grace and tenacity, and helped usher in the era of more equitable gender rights for female athletes for the remainder of the twentieth century.

Another African American sports giant of the 1950s and 1960s is a basketball player who many consider to be the greatest American sports champion of all time. Standing 6-feet 10-inches tall, Bill Russell was born in Monroe, Louisiana, in 1934, but grew up in Oakland, California. His family moved west in an attempt to avoid the racial animosity that existed in the American South in those days. Though it took Russell some time to add strength to his lanky frame, he became a star at the University of San Francisco (USF), budding into the greatest defensive player the sport had ever seen. Russell was unmovable in the low post, and after honing his skills on the offensive end of the court, he averaged more than twenty points and twenty rebounds per game, leading USF to two consecutive national championships in 1955 and 1956.

In the year of the second NCAA title, Russell represented U.S. basketball at the 1956 Summer Olympics in Melbourne, Australia. He led the Americans in scoring over eight games en route to a 34-point gold medal win over the Soviet Union. Later that year, Russell joined the Boston Celtics of the National Basketball Association, continuing his championship run by helping the team to the 1957 NBA title over the St. Louis Hawks, pulling down thirty-two rebounds in the decisive Game 7 of the NBA Finals. During thirteen seasons, Russell helped Boston amass eleven NBA championships, including an astonishing run of eight straight from 1959 to 1966. Bill Russell was the epitome of hard work and honorable sportsmanship, showing leadership as a player and NBA head coach. His numerous accomplishments as a winner might never be equaled again.

The final outstanding African American athlete to be thoroughly examined in this chapter stands out not only as an extraordinary champion of boxing, but may well deserve the accolade "Greatest of All Time" for his activities outside the ring. Born with the name of Cassius Clay in Louisville, Kentucky, in January 1942, Muhammad Ali is one of the rare human beings who transcended sports and has lived as a legend in his own time. Simultaneously the best at what he did as well as the most popular, Ali was to boxing what The Beatles were to music. In other words, there was never a time during Ali's career when he failed to capture the imagination of anyone who witnessed his talents in and out of the boxing ring.

At the age of eighteen, Ali (still known as Cassius Clay) took home the gold medal in boxing as a light heavyweight at the 1960 Rome Olympics. From that point forward, the only thing on his mind was earning a chance to fight for the heavyweight championship of the world, a moment that seemed predestined to the confident and charismatic Ali. He crafted a persona that came across as intentionally arrogant in a way that would disrupt the psyche of future opponents who wanted to take him down a notch.

By February of 1964, Ali had found the bull's-eye of his title-dream dartboard in the form of Sonny Liston, a bruising boxer who had dismantled champion Floyd Patterson in a first-round knockout to take the title in 1962. Ali used rhyming poetry and his flair for the television camera to taunt Liston, who dismissed the twenty-two-year-old as out of his league. Unfortunately for Liston, Ali (still Cassius Clay at the time) had the bite to back up his boasts, and at the start of the 7th Round, Liston quit, never rising from his corner stool, making Ali the second-youngest heavyweight champion of the world at the time. The day after the fight, Cassius Clay officially became Muhammad Ali.

Throughout the course of the 1960s, Muhammad Ali was the face of American sports and a voice of dissention who rattled the white establishment of the United States. Ali represented the Black Muslims, his new faith, and he was always a vocal proponent of equal rights, by any means necessary, for African Americans. For those who wanted to quiet the champion, there was nothing anyone could do. Ali's status grew larger with each heavyweight title defense around the globe that saw "The Champ" defend his belt eight times. Ultimately he was forced to give up the championship by a court order, after choosing to be a conscientious objector to the Vietnam War and refusing to be drafted.

Upon being reinstated in the 1970s, Muhammad Ali fought three iconic bouts against Smokin' Joe Frazier, including the "Thrilla in Manila," and developed the rope-a-dope fighting technique to defeat a previously unbeaten George Foreman in 1974 to regain his title after a seven-year gap. With ten more consecutive title defenses throughout the 1970s, Ali was arguably the greatest boxer, if not athlete, of the twentieth century. In his heyday, it was almost certain that Muhammad Ali's face would be recognized in any country in the world, from a small city in Peru to a mountainous village in the Himalayas. Because of the force of his personality and his skills in the boxing ring, it may be a long time before the world will see a single athlete so transcendent as Muhammad Ali.

As we conclude, other African American firsts of note include Willie O'Ree, who broke the NHL's color barrier while playing ice hockey for the Boston Bruins from 1957-1979; George Poage, who was the first African American to compete in the Olympic Games, which he did as a track & field athlete in the 1904 Summer Olympics in St. Louis; Charlie Sifford, who desegregated the PGA by playing in the 1952 Phoenix Open (via an invitation procured by boxing great

Joe Louis); and Sylvester Croom, who became the first black head coach of a Southeastern Conference (SEC) football team when he took over the Mississippi State University Bulldog program in 2003.

While many strides have been made concerning the integration and acceptance of African Americans as equal citizens and athletes worthy of blind comparisons to the sporting greats of any era, there still exists a discrepancy in modern athletics regarding the positioning of black men and women in prominent posts such as general managers and head coaches, with a vast number of these high-profile jobs going to white men. Thankfully, recent successes by such strategic tacticians as head coaches Tony Dungy, who led the Indianapolis Colts and Peyton Manning to an NFL title by winning Super Bowl XLI in 2007, and Doc Rivers, who helped bring glory to the city of Boston by leading the Celtics to an NBA-best seventeenth championship in 2008, have shown that a person's race has little to do with the ability to rise to the top. Hopefully the future will hold more opportunities for African Americans to illustrate that the color of one's skin does not affect the power of one's mind or the capacity to lead others toward greatness in sports or anything otherwise. Only the narrow-minded will find reasons to exclude someone based on anything other than the content of his or her character.

6

Women's Involvement in Sports and Its Coverage

Equality is a concept that many people measure differently. Not surprisingly, the reality of such a notion is never something that truly matches the ideal form of the definition. In other words, things in life are never truly split fifty-fifty. As we discussed in the last chapter regarding racial bias, shifting the world so that prejudice and unfairness can be diminished to any extent is an ongoing task set on the shoulders of those willing to constantly push for change.

Such is the case for women's athletics, specifically in terms of "accepting" or even "allowing" females to take part in activities that men have participated in for thousands of years. Equally challenging has been the struggle for women to cover sports. This chapter will serve to outline and discuss the difficulties that have faced women in sports and sports reporting. The particular focus will be on the last forty years, when women in American athletics were finally given legislative support to receive federal funding for collegiate and high school competitive sports involvement. Therefore, let us return to the ancient past and work our way up to the point of Title IX in the 1970s, individually describing the groundbreaking women who have led us to the current state of women's sports in the twenty-first century.

As was mentioned in chapter 3 regarding the ancient Olympic Games held in Greece starting in 776 BCE, women were prohibited from competing in or even watching the events. In fact, the first Olympic award given to a female, whose name was Princess Cynisca of Sparta, was bestowed on her because she was the owner and breeder of the horses that won the chariot race of those Games, not because she herself competed. This is not to say there weren't women participating in sports-related activities in ancient times. In fact, legendary Greek author Homer wrote in *The Odyssey* in 800 BCE about a character named Princess Nausicaa, who was playing ball with her handmaidens on the Island of Scheria when Odysseus and his men sailed to shore looking for a safe haven. Nausicaa was able to assist Odysseus in finding shelter, thus making her a significant character in the epic tale. But, more noteworthy than this, Nausicaa will go down in history as the first person ever, male or female, to be described in literature as playing a game with a ball. Additionally, the Elgin Marbles that once lined the Parthenon in Athens feature many carvings of Amazons, with women using athletic skills in combat.

True to the ancient tale of Princess Nausicaa, sports were primarily a recreational form of physical fitness for women for much of recorded history, with very few official athletic competitions taking place for females prior to the 1900s. Women still formed independent clubs to exercise with one another in a casual fashion, playing games such as tennis, croquet, bowling, and archery. These clubs became more official organizations for female students who wished to compete with their peers at some of the smaller universities in the northeastern United States, notably the Seven Sisters. Examples include women's basketball at Smith College in Northampton, Massachusetts, in 1892, and tennis tournaments between Bryn Mawr and Vassar Colleges in Pennsylvania and Poughkeepsie, New York, respectively. Vassar, an all-women's college at the time, was truly the forerunner for female sports in the nineteenth century, with athletic teams for students such as baseball, rowing, golf, and ice skating. These schools would hold intramural, "play day" events, which served as precursors to Title IX, the federal law that aimed at creating an equal footing for women and men in college and high school sports.

Sadly, despite the endorsement of women's sports by such early twentieth-century societies as the Committee of Women's Athletics (CWA), the American Physical Education Association (APEA), and the Girls Athletic Association (GAA), there was a prevailing mind-set that women had a limited amount of endurance at their disposal. Women, so the thinking went, were better off tending to more "ladylike" endeavors, to wit, raising children or keeping the home clean and tidy. In spite of these views, many women continued to play sports and fight for equal rights at various liberal arts colleges and schools, as well as universities such as Cal-Berkeley and Stanford. But just as momentum for women's rights began to build after the suffrage movement and the Nineteenth Amendment giving women the right to vote, the Great Depression of the 1930s hit. Sports equality for women was put on the backburner, and financial survival became primary.

On the heels of the Depression came World War II. And while it was devastating in almost every way imaginable, the war did kick-start numerous opportunities for women to advance in the workforce. With memorable contributions such as 1942's "Rosie the Riveter" song or J. Howard Miller's "We Can Do It!" poster, women and men alike formed new images of the working woman in society. They were depictions that showed that women were more than capable of holding their own and surely worthy of opportunities to compete in official sporting events.

The most notable example of a female sports association during World War II is an unforgettable, if not somewhat controversially sexist, variation of men's professional baseball that was chronicled in the 1992 film *A League of Their Own* starring Geena Davis, Madonna, and Tom Hanks. In fictional form, the hit comedy recounted the events surrounding the All-American Girls Professional Baseball League (AAGPBL). The league was founded in 1943 by Phillip K. Wrigley, whose family started the Wrigley's Chewing Gum Company, in addition to owning the Chicago Cubs. Wearing skirts instead of pants to show off a little skin (in hopes of heightening attendance and overall popularity), the AAGPBL consisted of eight Midwestern teams spanning 1943 to 1945, with names such as the Kenosha Comets, the Rockford Peaches, the Racine Belles, and the Grand Rapids Chicks. In all, the women's baseball league lasted until 1954, with a total of fifteen franchises fielding teams and more than six hundred women suiting up for game action. Surely, this experiment to form a women's baseball league was a successful endeavor—the games were played over the course of a decade. Besides giving Americans a sense of business-as-usual during wartime, the AAGPBL enabled women to show that they were capable of competing in athletic events that drew crowds. The torch was passed forward.

In the time spanning the Great Depression to almost a decade after World War II, one woman in particular stands out for her athletic accomplishments. Mildred Ella "Babe" Didrikson, who married and became known as Babe Didrikson Zaharias until her untimely death from cancer in 1956, was simply the greatest female athlete of the twentieth century, if not the overall best female competitor the world has ever seen. Didrikson dominated her peers in a multitude of sports throughout her life, first coming to prominence after taking home two gold medals in hurdles and javelin, and one silver, as a twenty-one-year-old competing in the 1932 Los Angeles Summer Olympics. Then, after World War II, Babe moved to golf with forty-one Ladies Professional Golf Association (LPGA) wins and ten major championships over the span of just nine years. So superb was Babe Didrikson that she was inducted into the World Golf Hall of Fame in 1951 while she was still in her prime. Didrikson was unstoppable on the basketball court as well, helping lead her team to the 1931 championship of the Amateur Athletic Union (AAU). In total, Babe Didrikson Zaharias was given the Associated Press Female Athlete of the Year Award six times, initially in 1932 and finally in 1954—a run of more than two decades of supremacy. It is a tragedy that Babe Didrikson Zaharias was only forty-five years old when she died.

Two athletes mentioned briefly in chapter 5 who were extremely significant to both women and African Americans across the United States in the mid-twentieth century were Wilma Rudolph and Althea Gibson. Wilma Rudolph, the speedster, was born in rural Tennessee in 1940. She contracted polio at age four, and wore leg braces and orthopedic shoes until she was a teenager because of the debilitating disease. Despite the ailment, Rudolph became a champion track star in high school, garnering a bronze medal at the young age of sixteen at the 1956 Summer Olympics held in Melbourne as a member of the 4x100–meter relay team. Then, after sprinting to a national champion at Tennessee State University and setting various records, Rudolph became the first African American female to take home multiple Olympic gold medals, capturing three of them at the 1960 Rome Summer Olympics. Those Games were the first televised to a worldwide audience, so Rudolph's popularity soared during and after the events. She earned nickname of The Tornado and became an exemplar of women's sports and a beacon for African American civil rights. She fought vehemently for equality after her running career was over. Rudolph was named Associated Press Female Athlete of the Year in both 1960 and 1961 before being enshrined in the U.S. Olympic Hall of Fame in 1993 and the Women's Hall of Fame in Seneca Falls, New York, in 1994.

Another African American female sports legend is Althea Gibson. She was the first person of color, male or female, to not only compete professionally in tennis, but to also become a Grand Slam champion, prevailing in the 1956 French Open at the age of twenty-eight. Using a graceful style that made her appear to be floating on the tennis court, Gibson was without equal for a three-year stretch, winning five Grand Slam singles titles from 1956 to 1958, including three of the four majors, Wimbledon, the U.S. Open, and the French Open. She claimed the Wimbledon and U.S. crowns in both 1957 and 1958, and was a finalist at the 1957 Australian Open. In doubles tennis, Gibson captured an amazing six additional Grand Slam titles in that same span, a feat that illustrates her dominance of the sport at the time. Like Wilma Rudolph and Babe Didrikson Zaharias, Gibson was given the Associated Press Female Athlete of the Year Award, with hers coming in 1958. Althea Gibson continued to contribute to numerous women's athletic organizations as a mentor and leader throughout her life. She was elected in 1980 to the International Woman's Sports Hall of Fame and was the 1991 recipient of the NCAA's Theodore Roosevelt Award, which specifically noted her "qualities of competitive excellence and good sportsmanship."

From the previous stories of individual achievement in women's athletics, we shift our focus to the organization that helped push for sporting equality, leading to the passage of Title IX in 1972. The Division for Girls' and Women's Sports of the American Association for Health, Physical Education, and Recreation, or DGWS, founded in 1941, became a precursor to the governing body that first oversaw collegiate women's athletics. In the 1940s, the DGWS began holding women's national golf championships on an annual basis, soon after incorporating other sports such as basketball, tennis, and track & field. As more and more women started to compete, additional organizations were formed to oversee the competitions. Although there were a few loose networks of affiliation, unlike men, college women did not compete with each other nationally. A three-pronged Tripartite Committee of groups focused on women's physical fitness and monitored events in various geographical regions of the United States. In 1957, they merged to become the National Joint Committee on Extramural Sports for College Women, or NJCESCW. Finally, in 1965, the NJCESCW turned the reins back over to the DGWS, which established the CIAW, or Committee on Intercollegiate Athletics for Women, a group that fashioned the framework for modern collegiate women's sports, sponsoring national championships under the auspices of the DGWS.

The scaffolding had been molded, secured, and structured in such a way to allow for general acceptance and official recognition. Next began the legal buildup toward gender-based competitive athletic equality in the eyes of the United States government.

The Association for Intercollegiate Athletics for Women, or AIAW, was created in 1971 out of the CIAW, creating a tight-knit alliance that operated on a national level with elected representatives and a board of trustees. One of its objectives was to illustrate its legitimacy and seriousness in obtaining government funding for women's athletics. But a revolution is always an evolution, and the march toward Title IX was a uphill climb, finally being put into a higher gear with the passage of the 1964 Civil Rights Act and 1967's Executive Order 11375, both during the presidency of Lyndon Baines Johnson. These two legislative actions prohibited any federal discrimination based on race or gender for things such as voter registration and employment conditions. It took an amendment to the 1964 Civil Rights Act to bring about gender equality in athletics. With the stewardship of Senator Birch Bayh and Representative Edith Green in 1972, the Educational Amendment to the Higher Education Act of 1965 was expanded as follows: *"No person in the United States shall, on the basis of sex, be excluded from participation in, be denied the benefits of, or be subjected to discrimination under any education program or activity receiving federal financial assistance."* In this statement, "activity" included sports.

With this, Title IX was born, and the future was unalterably changed. The amendment meant that any American college, university, or high school receiving any federal government support, which nearly every one was, could have the entirety of that funding stripped clean if the school failed to comply with the federal mandate. Shortly after the law was signed by President Richard Nixon on June 23, 1972, the AIAW quickly expanded to include 280 academic institutions across the United States, and the game was on. Next was the question of a merger between the women's organization group and the previously unchallenged NCAA, which controlled all male sports and had opposed diverting funds from men's programs to women's. The NCAA initially felt this was all a big waste of people's time and money, but the AIAW was ready to compete on an equal plane. Thus began, in earnest, the push to see whether women belonged in a world of sports dominated by men, and belong they did.

Throughout the 1970s, women's collegiate and high school athletics increased at a steady pace, as the Department of Housing, Education, and Welfare (HEW) oversaw the implementation of Title IX. By 1981, the AIAW hosted national championships for college women in nineteen sports, including basketball, field hockey, golf, gymnastics, track & field, soccer, softball, swimming, diving, and volleyball. Some sports such as basketball weren't merely financially solvent, but were able to turn a profit during its Final Fours, with championships taking place in New York City's Madison Square Garden in 1975. Noting the upward trend of incoming money for women's athletic events, the NCAA chose to begin offering its own versions of AIWA's national championships. In 1982, some of the country's most prominent women's basketball programs, Old Dominion, Louisiana Tech, and Tennessee, jumped ship and joined the financially colossal NCAA, essentially putting an end to the AIAW forever. Though AIAW chose to officially disband in 1983 after a court ruling favored the NCAA, its influence on pushing women's athletics into the realm of legitimacy was more than significant. Without the organization, many of the female sports stars of today would never have had a chance to be seen by national television audiences or taken seriously as competitors.

Speaking of the measurement of man versus woman in sporting competition, there is no better illustration of a trailblazer and laudable contributor to female athletes everywhere than the tennis champion Billie Jean King. In a career that saw King amass a whopping twelve Grand Slam singles victories (including six Wimbledon titles and four U.S. Open championships) as well as twenty-seven additional Grand Slam doubles titles for thirty-nine career Grand Slam wins, King is best known for her 1973 defeat of male tennis star Bobby Riggs in a staged but fully competitive singles event held at the Houston Astrodome. The buildup for the match was like that for a championship prize fight, with Riggs running his mouth like a professional wrestler, saying that a woman could never beat a man, even on his worst day. He believed his boast after defeating Wimbledon champion Margaret Court in straight sets earlier that year. The banter captured the imagination of the American public, and before a crowd of more than thirty thousand and a worldwide televised audience approaching forty million viewers, King dispatched Riggs in methodical straight-set fashion, winning 6-4, 6-3. King, always courteous and dignified, has gone on to maintain a constant presence as a commentator for hundreds of professional tennis events. In 1973, *Sports Illustrated* named King Athlete of the Year and in 1987, she was inducted into the International Tennis Hall of Fame.

Before the close of the 1970s, many women had performed with excellence in a variety of sports. One of the best in basketball was Ann Meyers, whose married name is Meyers Drysdale. A proficient athlete for all of her life growing up on the West Coast, Meyers flourished on the basketball court in high school, so much so that she became the first scholastic member of the U.S. National Women's Basketball team and the first-ever female athlete to earn a full four-year paid athletic scholarship, awarded by UCLA. In Los Angeles, Meyers showed her ball skills on a daily basis, recording a quadruple-double in one game in 1978 (twenty points, fourteen rebounds, ten assists, and ten steals) before leading her team to the AIAW national championship later that year. As if Meyers hadn't done enough already to prove that women were worthy of athletic equality, she became the first (and only) woman to sign a professional NBA contract, penning a $50,000 deal with the Indiana Pacers for the 1980–'81 basketball season (unfortunately, she did not make the team after tryouts). Now a member of multiple Halls of Fame, Meyers Drysdale has served as a television broadcaster for NBC's coverage of the 2000 Summer Olympics, and is currently acting as president and general manager for the Women's National Basketball Association's (WNBA's) Phoenix Mercury and as a vice president for the NBA's Phoenix Suns. Tell Ann Meyers Drysdale she can't do something, and it's already finished.

Regarding women playing prominent roles in sports broadcasting, the latter portion of the twentieth century ushered in an era of equality in the media-rich twenty-first century, where women including Doris Burke routinely call men's basketball games (as well as women's) for ESPN, and Beth Mowins takes the microphone in a play-by-play role for ESPN college football coverage. Along with names such as Pam Ward, Rachel Nichols, Bonnie Bernstein, Mary Carillo, Phyllis George, Robin Roberts, Lisa Salters, Hannah Storm, Lesley Visser, Erin Andrews, and Michele Tafoya, women are proving that a female voice during any time of televised sports broadcast is just as natural as the sound of a cheering crowd, and is something to be treated with ordinary enjoyment and not as any type of experimental novelty.

In the last decade-plus on the international stage, U.S. women's athletics have been led mainly by the U.S. women's soccer team. Among the notable moments was Brandi Chastain's penalty kick to win the 1999 Women's World Cup. Brilliantly skilled players such as Abby Wambach and Alex Morgan, among others, showed that women are equally capable athletes as men. In Olympic sports, women continue to achieve fame on a worldwide scale, with star-turning performances such as Lindsey Vonn's 2010 gold medal in downhill skiing in Vancouver or Gabby Douglas's all-around gymnastics gold in the 2012 London Olympics, placing them among the country's all-time greats. On the collegiate level, women's basketball now sees players including Baylor University's Brittany Griner dunking on a regular basis as well as million-dollar television contracts for the NCAA women's basketball tournament. The notion that female athletics is somehow less important or disproportionately worthy of admiration is fading. What the future holds is anyone's guess, but there is no doubt that women and sports are a mix that will continue to increase in importance and prevalence over the coming decades.

7

Amateur Athletics in the United States

As the saying goes, amateurs do something until they get it right; professionals do it until they can't get it wrong. Technically speaking, amateur sport participants compete in events for no monetary rewards. Most of the time they play and gain experience in hopes of becoming professionals and cashing a paycheck for their hard-earned work. Despite the fact that amateur athletes do not "play for pay," they are no less passionate about competing and performing under pressure. Sometimes winning alone is more than enough motivation, and this desire to succeed is one of the fundamental principles of amateur athletics, driving men, women, girls, and boys of all ages to pursue greatness in any type of sport in which they aim to excel. This fact exists in everything from junior Olympic trials all the way down to summer slow-pitch softball leagues. Amateur athletics are the backbone of a society's leisure activities, illustrating the innate need for gregarious competition and the desire to prove skill and rank in any type of sport.

In this chapter, we will conduct an examination of the most prominent amateur sports organizations in the United States, detailing the opportunities to compete that lie along the path toward a prospective professional career, touching on the statistical breakdown of the odds one faces as a young sports enthusiast with dreams of making the "Big Leagues" someday. In addition, this chapter will look at the expansion of media coverage of amateur sports in America, investigating the proliferation of new global communication outlets that have sprung up because of the reach of the Internet. Athletes in any professional league or sports association have undoubtedly participated in amateur sporting events in the early stages of their careers. Beyond that, local leagues and organized competitions provide an essential part of being a modern citizen who is able to practice and perform in sporting events together with and in front of their families and friends.

To begin, this textbook has thus far explained that sports have existed for thousands of years, and competitive events have enthralled spectators and been recorded in some form of media since the dawn of ancient times. In addition, sports have constantly been accompanied by the benefit of some type of reward for the victorious person or team. Some historic societies went so far as to use athletics as a way of deciding who lives and who dies (the Roman Coliseum and gladiators instantly come to mind, as well as the Aztec sport of tlachtli played in 1000 BCE). Sport has and always will exist as a representation of war, or at least regional dominance in some way or another. That is the case whether the prize for victory is the right to live, an olive branch, or the gold-laden medals and trophies bestowed on our champions in the modern era: to the victor goes the spoils, even in sports that are considered to be "amateur."

What, then, does the word "professional" denote in terms of labeling an athlete a pro or not? Specifically, being a professional is defined as following an occupation as a means of livelihood for financial gain, as in the case of a professional musician or carpenter. In modern times, a pro sports player is quite easy to define, meaning that it is a person who takes home a paycheck of some sort (or "receives remuneration" for his or her services) for the public exhibition of remarkable athletic expertise. This payment can be in the form of direct prize money for winning an event, as with PGA or LPGA golfing tournaments, or via a contractual agreement between an athletic franchise and the player (a deal brokered almost always by a lawyer, known as a sports agent, who is familiar with the legal aspects of the arrangement). Another mode of payment is through corporate or business-related sponsorship, which happens quite often in smaller-revenue sports such as motocross or extreme sports like skateboarding or BMX bicycle racing. Of course, numerous professional athletes (the most successful ones, specifically) are able to find financial rewards from any of the three categories listed above—in many instances, they gain income from each one of these sources. Without revenue from commercial endorsements, countless athletes would have little chance of continuing their athletic pursuits, let alone obtaining the astronomically high salaries many earn annually.

Still, there is nothing like playing sports for the pride and honor of being victorious. One example of amateur athletics that instantly comes to mind for most Americans is Little League Baseball, which is supervised on an official level by Little League Baseball Incorporated (a company that also goes by the name Little League International Baseball and Softball). Founded in 1939 by a man named Carl Stotz, the organization was started in Williamsport, Pennsylvania, with the intent of encouraging people to volunteer to support the formation of youth baseball leagues across the country. Today, there are more than 200,000 Little League teams across the globe from over one hundred nations and in almost every single town in America. An estimated 2.6 million boys compete in baseball and more than 500,000 girls play youth softball annually worldwide. The Little League World Series, which is held at the Howard J. Lamade Stadium in South Williamsport every summer, involves the sixteen best squads from around the world, with the championship broadcast to a national television audience on ESPN.

Perhaps the greatest reason for the success of the Little League World Series lies in the fact that so many boys and girls have participated in youth baseball over the last seventy-plus years, with everyone holding dreams of reaching the glory of a title. Another cause could be the way baseball experts look to scout future talent, allowing Little League Baseball to serve as a springboard to high school stardom and then possibly to the Major Leagues. Statistics aside, it's almost guaranteed that every professional baseball player took part in Little League Baseball at some point in his life. And it's not outside the realm of possibility that a Little League World Series player makes it to the Big Leagues. In fact, it has happened dozens of times, with names like Gary Sheffield, Dwight Gooden, Tom Paciorek, and Jason Marquis making the exclusive list.

Briefly mentioned in chapter 6, the Amateur Athletic Union (AAU) has been a mainstay in American sports since 1888, when it was established by William Buckingham Curtis in New York City. The AAU still exists in the twenty-first century, and it holds yearly amateur championships such as the AAU Junior Olympic Games, allowing youth and young adults ages sixteen to twenty-three to participate in more than thirty different sports and team events. The AAU also helped spawn the United States Olympic Committee in 1894 (to be discussed shortly). In total, the AAU oversees almost 500,000 participants and 50,000 volunteers, with thousands of teams playing sports such as AAU basketball each year in fifty-six districts across the country. Nearly every Division I NCAA basketball player takes part in an AAU basketball league at some point during his or her high school career. The AAU is essential to the growth and advancement of elite athletes in the United States.

Along the same governing-body lines as the AAU, each state in America has its own high school sports association, with acronyms abounding, such as the IHSA for Illinois and the MHSAA for the state of Michigan. Almost eight million students participate in high school athletics annually, which amounts to more than 55 percent of the entire student population for that age group. Basketball has the greatest number of high school teams in the United States, with more than 35,000 squads competing around the country each year, while football claims the throne as having the most individual high school participants, as more than 1.1 million boys suit up in pads and helmets each season.

Taking part in athletic competition is not merely beneficial for physical fitness. Various studies in recent years have shown that high school sport participants carry GPAs nearly one point higher than non-athletes. These students also miss fewer days of school and attend classes more frequently than non-athletes, and were more than 40 percent more likely to graduate from college than those who did not play sports. These figures not only suggest multiple benefits to playing amateur athletics, they give credence to the leadership, tenacity, and selfless dedication inherent in sports that help create success later in life. Amateur sports have broader benefits than solely winning trophies or going on to achieve professional success in sports, they offer an advantage for those willing to make a commitment to better their lives through organized competition and to devote time to official forms of athletics.

The United States Olympic Committee (USOC) is another immensely important amateur sports organization in America. Headquartered in Colorado Springs, the committee manages the Olympic Games, Paralympic Games, Youth Olympic Games, and Pan American Games. Its goal is to inspire sustained competitive excellence in the spirit of the Olympic movement. In total, the USOC organizes thirty-eight different summer and winter sports that are supervised by their own National Governing Body (NGB). Examples include USA Basketball, USA Gymnastics, USA Track & Field, U.S. Figure Skating, USA Hockey, and the United States Ski and Snowboard Association. Though it is a nonprofit organization, the USOC is no small fry, operating with an annual budget of more than $150 million. Furthermore, the USOC oversees the U.S. Olympic television coverage. A portion of the $4.38 billion contract from NBC Sports goes to the USOC for the network's coverage of the 2014, 2016, 2018, and 2020 Olympic Games. These are amateur sports, but they're also big business.

In terms of putting media coverage of amateur athletics into historical perspective, one of the first ever collegiate sporting events to be broadcast took place in 1912 at the University of Minnesota, when live updates of a Gophers football game were delivered via the telegraph by Professor F. W. Springer and his assistant H. M. Turner. The two men watched the game in person and sent out messages through an experimental, radio-type transmitter station going by the name of 9XI-WLB, which could theoretically be seen as the first Twitter account on Earth. Almost twenty years later, during the nascent years of radio in America, a football game between the universities of Pittsburgh and West Virginia was broadcast on November 5, 1921, making it the first time radio introduced amateur athletics to audiences. As we discussed in chapter 2, radio boomed to such overwhelming popularity in the 1920s that one in every three American families owned the device by 1929. With this, hundreds of collegiate athletic events were aired during the Golden Age of Sports of the 1920s. These broadcasts helped legendary players, such as Harold "Red" Grange of the University of Illinois and the Four Horsemen of Notre Dame, to become household names across the United States.

The 1930s brought the advent of television to the American public, with a broadcast of a baseball game played in New York City between Columbia and Princeton Universities the first game on the tube. In fact, the baseball game featured just one camera set stationary down the third-base line, which seems astoundingly rudimentary. It is interesting to note that sports broadcasting began with this amateur event between two Ivy League schools. The development and expansion of television was put on hold during World War II, but by the end of the 1940s, sports started being broadcast on local television channels. The 1948 Rose Bowl game streamed over the airways of Los Angeles–based KTLA, and in 1952, the Rose Bowl was aired to a national audience by NBC, and from this point forward, sports and television were interwoven with American culture.

During the second half of the twentieth century, other NCAA sports, particularly college basketball, gained an elevated role on television, especially during the March Madness tournament, which first tipped off in 1939. With an increased audience came more revenue dollars and expanded team invitations, pushing the original total from eight to thirty-two in the 1970s to sixty-four in 1985, all the way up to the current sixty-eight-team tournament. The men's tournament now is so successful that the average number of viewers over the course of the three-week event is more than ten million—with more than twenty-three million Americans watching the 2013 championship game between Louisville and the University of Michigan. The women's NCAA basketball tournament, which began in 1982, has also increased in viewership, with each of that event's games broadcast on ESPN's family of networks.

NCAA football is another enormously popular amateur sport, with a staggering thirty-five bowl games at the end of each season, culminating with the BCS National Championship Game held the second week of January each year (and the new four-team championship playoff slated to begin with the 2014 season). The college football title game consistently draws more than twenty-five million viewers each year, although only a fraction of the one-hundred-plus million people who watch the NFL Super Bowl each February. Still, college football is literally unavoidable on the airwaves during autumn Saturdays in America, with several dozen games shown live each week on networks including ESPN, ESPN2, ESPNU, CBS, NBC, ABC, Fox, FX, and Fox Sports, to name a few.

The topic of NCAA football bowl games is a good place to start when speaking about the seemingly paradoxical combination of amateur athletics and sports-based revenue. For instance, the U.S. Department of Education's Office of Postsecondary Education released a total related to Michigan State University's 2011–'12 school year athletic budget, which revealed that the university spent more than $19 million on the football team that season, bringing in revenue of $49.75 million. Most of this money came from television contracts. Critics of college sports ask, how is it possible for a sport that is officially "amateur" to turn a $30 million annual profit? Why aren't the players paid for their services? One side argues that the student athletes receive much in the way of reimbursement, with scholarship holders getting free tuition, room and board, meals, travel, and clothing. The superior athletes can also showcase skills that might yield a seven-figure NFL contract after departing school. The one counter argument is that the pretense of amateur in Division I major sports (principally football, basketball, and possibly hockey) should be reexamined, with players being paid salaries as school employees. A further wrinkle is a lawsuit about using players' images without pay, filed by former UCLA basketball player Ed O'Bannon against the NCAA. The suit in federal court has not yet been resolved, though two of the named defendants have settled—only the NCAA remains. No matter what one's opinions are regarding amateur athletics, it is quite certain that many of those participating in the bigger sports hope for professional careers and big salaries.

What, then, are the actual statistics related to a person's chances of hitting pay dirt in the pros when starting out as a high school athlete? To be blunt: not very good. In fact, of all high school football players in the United States, only 0.03 percent of them will make it to the NFL, and of the fifty-four thousand NCAA football players, only 0.6 percent of those top-tier athletes will rise to the highest level of the profession. For basketball, the numbers are quite similar, with 0.03 percent of high school boys getting a chance to play in the NBA, and only 1.2 percent of NCAA players making it to the professional league. Taking a step back from the professional ranks, only 3.2 percent of all American high school basketball players, boys and girls included, reach the level of playing for an NCAA team, yet every single person who has played basketball on a school yard blacktop or in a driveway has dreamed of hitting the winning shot in an NBA game, envisioning themselves smiling for the cameras and doing interviews for ESPN. Such is the nature of the human desire for success, and this lottery ticket mentality not only drives the dreams of the individuals who participate (as well as their parents), but has pushed a new realm of amateur sports media interest into the mainstream in the twenty-first century for anyone who follows a particular professional or university team.

Thanks to the pervasiveness of the Internet and the proliferation of smart-phones continuously hooked into the matrix of cyberspace, scouting talent for future basketball and football stars has become big business. Among the recruiting websites are Scout.com and Rivals.com, which have millions of daily readers and are both now corporately owned. Fox Sports bought Scout.com in 2005 for close to $50 million, and Yahoo! purchased Rivals.com in 2007 for $100 million. Mix in the explosion of social media outlets such as Twitter, and the chatter surrounding which particular university a highly regarded recruit might potentially choose to attend allows for sports talk to cycle continuously throughout the year. Rumors swirl on a daily basis, conjuring up hope and optimism in the minds of fan bases across the country.

Regarding networks, several television channels on cable and satellite services in the United States dedicate 100 percent of their programming to amateur athletics; more are surely on the way in the coming years. The pioneer of exclusive collegiate athletic content was CSTV, founded in June 2002 in New York City under the name National College Sports Network. After a rebranding as "College Sports Television," CSTV structured deals with satellite providers such as DirecTV to be the first independent cable network channel ever to reach a national audience. Its mainstays were sports such as NCAA soccer, football, and lacrosse. The idea was such a fast success that in 2005, CBS purchased CSTV for $325 million and, in conjunction with television broadcasts, began streaming content over the Internet. Fans could now pay subscription fees to watch live feeds of games that were never previously available. In 2011, CBS renamed the channel the CBS Sports Network, continuing to offer games online now for free, but with advertisements to bring in revenue. It is a monetizing business strategy that has become ordinary for almost every other sports network in the Internet and smartphone age.

Other well-known television channels that are exclusively devoted to amateur athletics, specifically to NCAA sports, include ESPNU, launched in March 2005, and the Big Ten Network, or BTN, which started showing conference-specific content in August 2007. This business approach has become the trend in recent times. The Pac-12 Conference started its own network in 2012 and the University of Texas at Austin's Longhorns Network created a channel showing only games of its team in 2011 as a partnership with ESPN. It is hard to imagine a day in the near future where every single Division I NCAA athletic conference doesn't operate its own network, whether it ends up existing on television, the Internet, or, most likely, both.

To conclude this chapter, other American amateur sports organizations of importance include the Pop Warner Little Scholars, also known as Pop Warner Football, which manages league games for boys ages five to sixteen in almost every state, with more than 450,000 youngsters hitting the gridiron every fall. Another is the American Youth Soccer Organization, or AYSO, which oversees amateur soccer leagues across the country, helping field 50,000 teams, with more than 600,000 players ages four through nineteen donning cleats and shin guards each year. The United States Golf Association, or USGA, is a more-than-century-old governing body that arranges both professional and amateur events for golfers in America. It sponsors the U.S. Amateur Championships, allowing citizens of this country of any age or gender to compete to be the best golfer in the nation. Winners of the event include Jack Nicklaus, Tiger Woods, and Bobby Jones, all of whom claimed more than one amateur title before going on to win handfuls of major professional golf championships.

Sports are integral to human culture worldwide, and the desire to compete is inspired much more by the sense of accomplishment than by the chase for riches and fame. Even though the remote possibility of a professional athletic career drives some parents to push their children into amateur athletics, the desire of most participants is to compete, improve abilities, and to have fun. From Pee Wee Football to AAU basketball, amateur sports are the indisputable gateway to professional athletic opportunities for young athletes, but they also teach people teamwork, provide leadership skills, and give individuals the means to find success in any number of lifetime undertakings.

8
Sports Media Ethics

Sports competitions bring joy and provide meaning to the lives of both competitors and fans, but what seems like mere fun and games can also exhibit a dark side. Journalists who cover sports are sometimes faced with reporting on the objectionable underside of the business, left to pull back the curtain to reveal truthful, but ugly, facts. The job of journalists is to dig into the layers of any newsworthy event, including sports, in order to uncover what is really going on, thereby allowing other individuals to assess the meaning and possible significance of such notable public incidents. The truth, however, is never a clear-cut proposition. The most fundamental job of a journalist is to report honestly on the activities witnessed, documents discovered, and on-the-record statements accumulated in the most accurate way possible. Truly, media ethics comes down to the concept of integrity, and this chapter will serve to explore the pertinent practices related to ethical conduct of sports and sports journalists in the United States.

Integrity is defined as the observance of moral and ethical principles, principally as they relate to honesty and unimpaired behavior on the part of a news reporter when linking this notion to journalism. Although conflicts of interest can exist in any type of journalism or news reporting, they are especially prevalent in sports reporting. A chief source of contention stems mainly from the fact that local sports journalists are almost always placed on a particular athletic beat. They follow the same team throughout the season and, in some cases, shadow a coach and related athletic program or organization for an entire career. In these familiar instances, it can be difficult for a journalist to fully disclose the complete set of facts regarding something scandalous or disreputable. The reporter may consequently worry more about displeasing personal acquaintances and possibly harming his or her status as a trusted contact within the group because of aggressive reporting. Such political concerns mean that sports journalists can unethically become willing mouthpieces of the sports program, athlete, or coach they were assigned to cover, thereby obstructing unbiased reporting, and ironically shielding society from the very truth the reporter was hired to reveal.

Recapping a sporting event and maintaining statistical accuracy is incredibly important, but at times there are circumstances within the sports world that have nothing to do with competition, and this is where ethics come into play for sports journalism. Athletes at any level can be role models, and with the millions, if not billions, of dollars at stake (with ancillary job possibilities attached to the success or failure of a franchise), reporting can ultimately affect a franchise. Sports hold a very real and prominent role in societies across the world, especially in America. Therefore, it is of utmost importance that a sports journalist exhibit the full spirit of integrity when working as a professional, simply because he or she owes it to the public at large as much as any other news reporter would.

Many scholarly works debating the principles of journalism point out that an essential task of reporters is to cause as little harm as possible, but the reality of life is that sometimes the truth hurts. Therefore, the question arises as to whether or not a story is helping by divulging the true information to counterbalance any potential damage. There must be a clear objective in mind when a story dealing with delicate or risky subject matter is being formulated in the mind of a reporter. The ultimate aim is to write a good story, yes, but beyond that, various values pertaining to conscience, morality, and the conceivable destruction of another person's character are imperative to consider before moving to make certain findings available to the public as a whole. The pen is indeed mightier than the sword, and a journalist's power to build up or destroy should not be taken lightly.

News reporters and sportswriters alike need to keep in mind that all of the facts are not always exposed at once, or in any sequential fashion. As a result, a story's various parts can sum up to something completely different from the final product with even one or two important puzzle pieces missing. On top of this, journalists should resist the temptation to publicize any bits of information gathered secondhand or via gossip or rumors through the grapevine. So many people are lured to release bits in the modern world of the Internet and social media, where information has a tendency to pour out spontaneously without fear of repercussion. If journalists are unsure about the authenticity of the information they have been given or have even tracked down themselves, they should not deliver that material to an open forum. It is simply an unfair and unethical method of reporting.

Before looking at some examples involving unethical behavior in athletic journalism or the handling of controversial issues in sports media, it is important to inspect some of the most common types of situations that are frequently encountered. The famous journalism scholars David H. Weaver and G. Cleveland Wilhoit wrote in their book *The American Journalist: A Portrait of U.S. News People and Their Work* that there are eight major categories of ethical dilemmas for news reporters to ponder when writing a story. These groups include (1) disclosing confidential sources, (2) using false information, (3) paying for confidential information, (4) using false identification (e.g., impersonating someone in order to trick someone else into disclosing what they think is being discussed in secret), (5) using personal documents without consent (e.g., spying on cell phone texts and reporting their content), (6) badgering sources (or being corrupt in terms of behavior related to threats or blackmail), (7) unauthorized use of confidential documents (e.g., what is being debated in current times with organizations such as WikiLeaks), and (8) undercover employment (e.g., getting hired at a job in order to acquire insider information without other people's knowledge).

If there is any theme to the above categories, it is that information should not be obtained surreptitiously and revealed without recognizing others' rights to privacy. Simply put, it is about maintaining integrity and staying true to principled values for any journalist. A reporter should follow his or her conscience when determining whether something is worthy of being uncovered, but, in the hopes of staying true to a core value system of principles, it must be stated openly that what *is* or *is not* ethical is seldom crystal-clear. There usually will be a gray area regarding what should or shouldn't be published, as well as which procedures are appropriate for obtaining particular details to get at what is seen as the truth. Furthermore, the "truth" is also a concept that is never 100 percent cut and dry, which therefore clouds the ability to define what specifically is or is not ethical. Such is the delicate nature of journalism.

In the quest of scrutinizing every angle of ethical news reporting, it is vital to now discuss what exactly is at stake for a journalist along every step of a career. What is this one item that can only be crafted slowly yet can be demolished in one single instant? The answer is *reputation*. In short, it represents a person's standing within the community in which he or she operates, big or small. In higher-profile cases, one's reputation can extend out into the public realm, affecting how a person is perceived and whether or not there is any merit to the work assembled and words written. Moreover, reputation can swing in either direction, which can occur when a news reporter is heralded for his or her ethical behavior and honest integrity, or conversely when errors in judgment and bad decision making render a person forever blacklisted as an unscrupulous and contemptible scoundrel who should never be trusted. Individuals have the opportunity to choose what type of reputation they want to construct for themselves, but there is much peril in damaging a reputation because it can never be fully restored after an unethical act. A bad reputation is the worst single characteristic one can possess in attempting to construct a lengthy, prosperous career as a journalist, sports included.

Therefore, each and every reporter needs to ask himself or herself, "What type of journalist do I want to be…someone who works hard and uses verified sources, conferring with colleagues or an editor whenever something scandalous might arise, or someone who cuts corners and publishes gossip and rumors, looking to expose secrets and smear good names for the sake of a popular story?" Being ethical has *nothing* to do with the content of a story, but everything to do with following one's conscience in hopes of adhering to the unwritten rules of morality that define a person whose conduct is unimpaired and rich with integrity. Injuring another person's reputation is a perfect way to damage your own.

Other types of unethical reporting methods consist of such rather obvious examples as plagiarizing someone else's work or fabricating information altogether, which has surprisingly occurred at some of the most prominent newspapers and magazines in America. In 1981, a *Washington Post* reporter named Janet Cooke was awarded the Pulitzer Prize for a 1980 story she filed about a young boy addicted to heroin which, though compelling, turned out to be completely fictional. Another notorious instance involved Stephen Glass, who falsified quotes and fabricated full stories for *The New Republic* magazine from 1995 to 1998. And then there was Jayson Blair, who was an up-and-coming journalist for *The New York Times* in 2003. Blair ruined his good name by lifting full news articles from other newspapers across the United States, plagiarizing or using falsified information in more than thirty of his seventy articles before his dishonesty was discovered and immediately halted. In each of these cases, each reporter's reputations were destroyed, never to be repaired. Their experiences are cautionary tales that should serve as a crucial lesson for any aspiring journalist. The competitive nature of news reporting can lead to temptations to cut corners, but acting with integrity provides its own rewards, especially as one sees his or her career grow in credibility and esteem.

Unethical practices in sports journalism, specifically, can be a bit harder to pin down, because there are varying degrees of what is or isn't appropriate when dealing with the perks and politics of the business. Should an embedded sports reporter write about any marital infidelity he witnesses out on the road while following a team for an extended period of time? Should a sportswriter accept handouts, such as covered travel expenses or complimentary tickets to games for friends and family, both of which could deter the reporter from wanting to tell the full truth about what is going on? What about conflicts of interest wherein a writer or television announcer plays favorites by being more of a public relations spokesperson filled with partiality rather than an objective journalist? As a response to these types of questions, the Associated Press provides editors with a list of ethical guidelines that explicitly prohibit such things as accepting money and gifts, clearly discourages conflicts of interest, and demands that writers do their own work in terms of seeking out information firsthand and reporting only on what they personally have found. Any quick analysis of these topics will lead to the conclusion that staying ethical and professionally responsible at all times can be challenging. A journalist always needs to ponder the risks and rewards when something includes the danger of putting his or her reputation in jeopardy.

A journalist's skill set requires that individual to record, summarize, and disseminate factual information to others (the who, what, when, where, and why), but there is also a second aspect of the job that incorporates the interpretation of whatever news events are being covered. This is where professionals need to understand the difference between being a reporter and a columnist, remembering that a journalist does not tell people *what* to think, but instead informs people on what to think *about*. For pure news distribution, such as sports recaps and write-ups, accurate depictions of observed evidence is all that is required, but in the case of being one who gives critical opinions as a columnist, there exists some leeway regarding the right for the author to editorialize details and offer personal views, attitudes, and outlooks.

More than ever, sports journalism in the twenty-first century combines both news and entertainment, so the line between reporter and columnist is easily blurred, as are many of the important concepts of this chapter. There will always be an element of craft associated with the art of writing and news reporting. Sometimes, however, a piece can venture into the territory of tabloid journalism if a writer is not careful, since gross exaggerations of actual events can turn the facts into caricatures of their true selves. Once again, it comes down to the morality and ethical nature of each individual to determine what is appropriate conduct when working in news media. The reputable journalist never forgets that this digital age in which we live is a place where words and opinions are etched forever in time. Pondering every move carefully is a crucial obligation for every aspiring journalist.

At this juncture, it seems appropriate to examine several cases of sports reporting that have involved scandalous subjects that required the reporter to dig out details judged to be worthy of public exhibition. In the area of investigative journalism, reporters are driven like detectives to solve mysteries by piecing the story together bit by bit, meticulously, one step at a time, over the course of weeks, months, or sometimes years. This impulse is a calling for some, as they are motivated by a desire to uncover the truth as a civic duty to others in the community or entire nation.

One recent example of investigative journalism in sports was conducted by Charles Robinson and Jason Cole of Yahoo! Sports, who began probing the off-the-field affairs of the University of Southern California's Heisman Trophy–winning running back Reggie Bush in 2005. The investigation revealed that Bush not only had taken monetary perks during the Trojans' BCS Championship run in 2004, but had received a six-figure amount of money used to purchase his mother a home, all well outside the boundaries for an amateur collegiate athlete. The Yahoo! Sports reports set off an NCAA investigation that ended in a lengthy probation for USC football, as well as the forfeiture of the university's 2004 national championship. At the same time the Reggie Bush scandal was revealed, Barry Bonds' story of steroid abuse throughout the later (and most prosperous) portion of his career was unearthed by San Francisco Chronicle reporters Mark Fainaru-Wada and Lance Williams. During their investigation of Bonds throughout 2004, the reporting duo learned of a complex doping routine for Bonds and other prominent track athletes from the "sports nutrition" firm BALCO. Culminating in the best-selling book *Game of Shadows*, which was released in March 2006, Bonds' legacy was forever stained, and his exit from Major League Baseball followed soon thereafter. Reporter David Walsh doggedly pursued Tour de France champion Lance Armstrong, contending that the All-American cycling hero and cancer survivor was enhancing his performance with banned substances through Walsh's reporting for the *Sunday Times*, and in his book *L.A. Confidential*, Walsh faced scathing attacks from Armstrong, including a libel suit that was decided in the cyclist's favor. Ultimately, Armstrong was unmasked and Walsh prevailed.

Other examples of investigative reporting include the point-shaving basketball scandals at Arizona State and Northwestern Universities, who in 1994 and 1995, respectively, had men's basketball players take payoffs to intentionally have the team miss baskets, thereby covering Las Vegas betting lines. Another infamous instance surrounded star New York Yankees third baseman Alex Rodriguez, whose history of steroid use while playing for the Texas Rangers from 2001 to 2003 was made public by Selena Roberts and David Epstein of *Sports Illustrated* in February 2009. To this day, A-Rod has never been able to live down the suspicion of performance-enhancing drug use, and his likelihood of making it into the MLB Hall of Fame in Cooperstown, New York, is in serious jeopardy. In each of these cases, journalists made the determination that the information gathered and shared was more beneficial to the public than it was harmful to the individuals affected by the scandals. These examples illustrate ethical journalism at its finest, carried out by risk-taking reporters willing to ask tough questions and demand truthful answers.

The world of sports will never be without its share of controversy. Television programs such as ESPN's *Outside the Lines* are at the forefront of investigative sports journalism in the twenty-first century, but there is also an epidemic of unprincipled, unethical reporting taking place via the numerous blogs and Twitter accounts that feed off of gossip and funnel rumors into the mainstream. Sadly, that content is given entirely too much credence by the 24-hour news cycles that demand fresh information on a continual basis. It is up to the individual journalist to determine what exactly he or she considers to be a legitimate sports story, which methods are utilized to gather information, and what details are placed into the public sphere. Reporters wanting to achieve greatness in the field of journalism must recognize that a solid foundation needs to first be constructed via hard work and resolute integrity. A good reputation is solidified by a steady output that represents the best attributes of a standout news reporter. Everyone's career moves at different speeds and in many various directions, but one thing is for certain: people will always remember exactly how one did or did not achieve success. A journalist's life is its own story.

9

The Business Side of Sports

Sports can be played in surroundings with no one watching and still mean as much to those participating as in any other competitive event. But, because the ultimate goal of competition is to win at the highest level possible, there is nothing like raising the stakes to the point where a victory can alter someone's career in a profoundly substantial fashion. Throughout history there have been instances where winning or losing in athletics determined life or death, but in the modern world, the most consequential reward is cold, hard cash. This fact means that sports is big business, especially in the twenty-first century. Several professional sporting leagues and franchises in America have revenues of multiple billions of dollars, with dozens more leagues functioning on hundreds of millions. Without the business side, sports would have less impact on societies around the globe, where winning or losing affects everything from television contracts to possible layoffs for minimum-wage workers. Professional and amateur athletics alike are indeed inseparable from various multifaceted financial interests. In America, they provide a significant social value, coalescing communities and delivering a tangible rooting interest where people cheer for their teams and invest in them financially as well as emotionally.

The best place to start when discussing sports and business is to describe the symbiotic relationship between athletics and the media, for it can be so obvious that it remains hidden from recognition. In the most basic sense, these two factions, sports and the media, need each other in every way possible when it comes to generating revenue and piquing public interest from season to season. The connection linking sports and the media is that of the yin and yang, where both fit like puzzle pieces into one another. Fan attention and enthusiasm yield advertising dollars for the media and revenues for the leagues, franchises, and teams, which helps to strengthen all parties involved. Yes, sports can exist in its own hidden spots around the globe, but when discussing sports business, the media is invariably running alongside, in step every moment of the day throughout the year, 24/7.

What, then, specifically, does professional sports possess that enables the industry to yield such large sums of monetary income on a continual (and contractual) basis? How can deals in the tens of billions of dollars between media entities and various leagues and organizations last for upwards of a full decade or more? The answer is a combination of exclusive distribution rights to live sporting events and the re-airing of programming on an unlimited basis. Each rebroadcast allows the network to reap advertising revenue from numerous commercial sources during breaks and in between broadcasts. There is also revenue from ticketing and merchandising for in-person viewing of games and matches. Taken as a whole, some of the current stats on the economics of sports broadcasting are astonishing.

For instance, in 2012, the Los Angeles Dodgers of Major League Baseball signed a twenty-five-year, $8 billion contract with Time Warner Cable (outbidding previous carrier Fox Sports West in the process) that will give exclusive rights to the newly formed SportsNet LA network, starting in 2014. SportsNet LA will transmit Dodger games to all cable and satellite subscribers in the region, as well as maintain a constant web presence with video updates and exclusive team access. The projected advertising revenue is expected to surpass the billion-dollar contractual fee shelled out by Time Warner for games to be beamed directly to the nearly eighteen million people in the Los Angeles metropolitan area. It is a testament to the longevity and consistent popularity of athletics that a corporation would be willing to strike such a long-term deal with a sports franchise—and the Dodgers' big TV contract is hardly one of a kind. All over the sporting world, teams in any size market are a prime commodity in fetching large advertising dollars. This is especially true in the modern era of Internet convergence, where a network is also given rights to control what is broadcast online and over smartphones, and where more ad revenue is accrued with every live stream or video clip watched.

Some teams such as the New York Yankees have their own personal network, as is the case with the YES Network, broadcasting out of New York City. Formed in 2002, the YES Network had an estimated value of $1 billion in 2004. In 2012, Rupert Murdoch's News Corp (owner of the Fox Networks and the *Wall Street Journal,* among other media outlets) purchased a 49 percent stake in YES for $3 billion. That is what investors call a positive return on a deal. In addition, the newest development in athletic broadcasting is for collegiate conferences to have their own networks and Internet websites devoted to team-specific events for their region of the United States. The Big Ten Network launched as a TV channel in 2007 and covers games for the conference, which increased from twelve to fourteen teams with the addition of Rutgers University and the University of Maryland in July of 2014. This expansion lets the conference gain access to the highly populated East Coast television markets that will boost the network's ratings and add to the Big Ten Conference's revenue.

Along these lines, in 2012, the Pac-12 Network became available on television and the Internet to West Coast college sports fans. The conference network established itself as the hub for present and past sports media content from USC, UCLA, Oregon, Stanford, and the rest of the teams from that sector of America. There is no foreseeable limit to the potential heights of sports media broadcasting via radio, television, and the Internet throughout the twenty-first century. The increasing draw of professional and amateur athletics from the last century ensures the media-related growth will continue. People will always love their favorite sports teams, passing that devotion on to future generations, whose thirst for more and more athletic content will surely be similarly insatiable.

The commercialization of sports is nothing new to this modern age of technology. Before mass communication, events were promoted and staged to the largest paying audience possible, offering up proceedings that could be witnessed only by those fortunate enough to obtain a ticket. Earlier in this book, we talked about heavyweight champion boxer Jack Johnson and his "Fight of the Century" in July 1910. That matchup was seen live by more than twenty thousand fans in Reno, Nevada, and was covered and written about by thousands of newspapers in the United States. This is an example of sports becoming such an integral part of American society, and it led to an increase in everything from stadium sizes to the speed at which information is disseminated and shared among the public.

These days, a venue such as AT&T Stadium in Arlington, Texas, home of the Dallas Cowboys of the NFL, is able to accommodate more than 105,000 fans during events, with room for thousands more to watch on large-screen HDTVs outdoors. A recent example of the interplay between fans in the seats and those watching nearby was Super Bowl XLV in 2011, when the Green Bay Packers defeated the Pittsburgh Steelers. Even if the fans could not be in the stadium, they were very close at hand for the championship game experience, shelling out hundreds of dollars just to stand outside. It is worth mentioning that the arena was named Cowboys Stadium up until 2013, when AT&T paid for the right to have its name on the building, and to be the primary sponsor of the NFL team. Particular numbers were not released regarding the Cowboys-AT&T deal, but similar stadium sponsorships run in the area of $20 million per year. With a franchise as valuable as the Dallas Cowboys, whose estimated worth was $2.1 billion as of 2012 (the richest in all American sports), the dollar amount of the AT&T deal is surely extravagant.

In a novel twist on the funding of a professional sports franchise, the NFL's Green Bay Packers began selling shares of their organization to the public as a way of keeping ownership of the team in the community where it was founded. By going public, the Packers effectively guaranteed that the team would not leave Green Bay. That hasn't been the case with other NFL teams: the Baltimore Colts relocated to Indianapolis in 1984, and the original Cleveland Browns moved to Baltimore and became the Ravens in 1996. Earlier, the Cardinals moved from St. Louis to Phoenix, having started in Chicago in the 1920s. The Rams and the Raiders have bounced around California, with the Rams finally landing in St. Louis.

In the case of the Packers, the team conducted a sale of stock, available to anyone living in Wisconsin in 1997 and 1998. Part of the proceeds funded renovations to historic Lambeau Field, where Green Bay has hosted football games since 1957. The Packers, who operate in the smallest market of any NFL team, yet hold multiple Super Bowl championships, were able to raise in excess of $24 million after issuing more than 100,000 shares at $200 apiece. Then, in a two-month span from December 2011 to February 2012, the team sold an additional 250,000 shares at a new price of $250 each. With almost five million shares in existence, this places the team's public value at close to $1.25 billion. Under the public ownership rules, shares may not be sold for profit, prohibiting a personal capital gain. Citizens are free to sell their stock back to the organization to recoup their initial purchase, but any profit to the team caused by increased share price is put into an account used to fund various charitable organizations across Wisconsin. In addition, in order to ensure that ownership of the Packers is widely dispersed among the community, no one person or business can own more than two hundred shares at one time, a regulation that enables the Packers to stay true to the vision of public ownership.

The popularity of sports makes athletics a valuable economic resource in so many different ways that this chapter could literally be expanded into its own book. The financial statistics connected with sports-related revenue are astounding. In 2012, according to *Forbes* magazine, the sports merchandising industry sold more than $12 billion worth of licensed goods in the United States for the third consecutive year in a row, after peaking at just over $15 billion in 2006. Imagine the thousands of jobs associated with the design, production, marketing, advertising, public relations, and distribution of something as simple as a team-licensed T-shirt. Then extend that out to anything that has a sports logo on it for any professional, collegiate, or, in these modern times, even high school athletics. There are team pajamas, team iPhone covers, team blankets, team wallpaper, team cookware, team pens and pencils, team sunglasses, team hats, shorts, skirts, tank tops, flip flops, water bottles, and anything else that has the ability for a logo to be stamped or stuck onto it. There is even a wrapping for the full body of a car or truck. Out of every officially licensed good sold, some portion of that revenue is going back to the organization, franchise, league, or conference associated with the product.

The business side of sports has gone so far that the Boston Red Sox offer officially licensed caskets for burial—lifelong devotion carried into the afterlife. Sports affiliation has created an entire industry based solely on the sale of licensed team merchandise that has proven to be sustainable with a solid future.

Money and athletics combine at the collegiate level as well. Among some Division I NCAA universities, revenue streams in the size of eight and nine figures are sizeable economic forces as well. In 2012, the most profitable collegiate sports program in America was at the University of Texas at Austin. The UT program topped the charts in total expenditures and revenue, with $138 million and $163 million, respectively, for that calendar year. Other universities that have massive athletic department budgets with nine-digit revenue intakes include Ohio State University ($142 million), the University of Michigan ($140 million), the University of Alabama ($125 million), and the University of Florida ($121 million). Revenue does not always guarantee profit, however. Expenses for operating the sports programs may outpace or just break even. Among eight other universities that turned at least some profit, Penn State took in $108,252,281 in 2012 and spent $107,389,258, a return of only $863,203, or 0.803 percent. For all of college athletics, there was more than $4 billion in combined revenue for the top two hundred teams. This figure validates the immense popularity of collegiate sports in America and the commensurate media presence that survives financially alongside them.

To offer another example, Michigan State University's sports program totals for 2012 included $81 million in revenue and $67 million in expenses, a profit of $13.5 million that represents a 20 percent plus-side return. Athletic department profits are important in sustaining collegiate sports, as most universities do not provide any money from the general fund. College football serves as the most expensive sport for any major university in America, with the Michigan State Spartan football program taking in just over $45 million, more than half of the entire athletics budget, with expenses at $17.4 million. There is very little doubt, based on the official figures released by the universities, that NCAA Division I college football is a breadwinner for dozens, if not hundreds, of schools across the United States. Some universities make a profit, while many break even, and others supplement athletics budgets from tuition and general fund dollars.

The Southeastern Conference (SEC) has arguably been the home of the top college football teams in recent decades, especially with universities from that conference holding seven of the last eight NCAA Football Championships. Consequently, and not coincidentally, in May 2013, the SEC dispersed a staggering $289 million in revenue to its fourteen teams—more than $20 million each. The infusion of funds is a way of keeping the programs at full strength, allowing them to seek out and secure commitments from the top high school football recruits around the nation. To put this into perspective, the SEC paid out $4.1

million to its schools in 1980, and didn't crack the $100 million barrier until 2003. Just ten years later, this revenue number has nearly tripled, which equals a 7,000 percent gain since 1980, meaning that revenue values have increased seventy-fold in slightly more than thirty years. This, again, is what economists and business experts alike would call an upward trend.

On the professional level, the business side of sports takes an even bigger spot in the fiscal composition of the American economy. The NFL is the largest of all professional leagues in the United States, with a current combined total worth of more than $30 billion for all thirty-two teams, according to a 2012 study by *Forbes* magazine. In addition, annual revenue per team is north of $250 million, with the Dallas Cowboys operating under the largest budget and reaping a revenue of half a billion dollars in 2012. To underscore the relationship between the media and any sporting organization, the NFL had, by far, the largest television contract of any American sports league, with more than $5 billion in annual revenue from Fox, CBS, NBC, ESPN, and the NFL Network (in contracts stretching into the year 2022). It is a figure that stands more than three times greater than that of the nearest competitor, Major League Baseball whose contracts gross over more than $1.5 billion per year.

As the NFL's annual overall revenue adds up to more than $9 billion, a total that has been rising steadily over the past few years, other major sports franchises are also financially healthy, though they do make less on a slightly fractional basis. Still not a strikeout by any stretch, Major League Baseball hauled in more than $7 billion in revenue in the year 2010, making it the second-largest sports association in the United States. The NBA, whose television revenue for 2012 was higher than $900 million, comes in as the third-largest league in America, operating with a revenue stream of almost $4 billion in 2010, which leaves the National Hockey League in the fourth spot, with a 2010 revenue of $2.7 billion.

Before addressing further areas of sports business, such as individual athlete sponsorships and advertising endorsements, as well as the business of sports agents and lawyers involved in professional sports negotiation, it is relevant to discuss one other piece of the sports business puzzle. That slice of the athletic economic pie involves sports unions and the representation by one single governing body of athletes in the various professional sports leagues across our country. The unions exist to keep an eye on the best interests of the players, offering up a unified public voice of solidarity vis-à-vis the team owners and CEOs, whose interests are primarily the team operation and profits.

As in any other industry, there are competing interests: employer and worker. With professional athletics, it is harder to decide what constitutes economic fair play. No one can claim that sports unions are in existence for purely altruistic intentions. For instance, the National Football League Players Association (NFLPA) negotiated the current NFL collective bargaining agreement (or CBA) in 2011, which will last until 2020, and had an operating budget in the hundreds of millions of dollars based on the annual fees of $10,000 per player. That dues figure currently sits at $15,000 per athlete, per year. It is a sizeable amount, given that there are more than 1,800 professional players in the NFL each season. The NFLPA ensures that players receive salaries that constitute a fair and equitable wage, especially for young players and veterans. Similar to the NFLPA, the NBA union is known as the National Basketball Player's Association (NBPA), and it also serves as the collective bargaining agent for the NBA's players, with annual dues required. In fact, recent in-fighting among the NBPA's members has seen a lawsuit filed by former player and head of the union Billy Hunter, who is seeking remuneration in excess of $10 million after he was essentially forced out of his position in 2011 for questionable investment deals over the previous decade. Other sports leagues' unions include the Major League Baseball Players Association (MLBPA) for professional baseball players and the National Hockey League Players' Association (NHLPA) for hockey players in America and Canada. It is of worth to note that each of these big four organizations has been in one or more labor disputes over the last two decades, with examples such as the cancellation of the 1995 World Series in baseball and the elimination of the entire 2004–05 NHL season.

To conclude this chapter dealing with the business side of sports, note that there is nothing inherently financial about the phenomenon of physical competition. However, with the goal being to win and defeat an opponent, it makes sense that there are so many billions of dollars up for grabs in the world of modern athletics. Without a doubt, money (or the symbolic representation of it) has served as an essential measure of one's rank and status in life for thousands of years. Putting together money, status, and athletic competition makes the significance of sports in our culture clear. Without the money involved in sports, people would still care about the outcome of any particular event. However, with billions of dollars changing hands on an annual basis, organized athletics has created an economic industry that is a driver of hundreds of thousands of different jobs in the United States every year.

10

Sports Agents, Endorsements, and Advertising

What would sports be without the allure of big money and famed celebrity status to anyone who has ever achieved some measure of success on the playing field at one point or another? Vast numbers of people in this world have participated in some type of sporting event, and no doubt, many have dreamed that their athletic accomplishments might lead to greener pastures of economic prosperity. For the average participant, and frankly for nearly 99 percent of those who play, images of athletic greatness are relegated to the realm of the imagination. Kids in a driveway count down the clock before swishing the NBA championship–winning bucket, or players on a golf course imagine they're lining up to sink the winning putt to secure a Master's green jacket. We can all dream, but that's usually as far as our athletic achievements extend.

In today's world, those select few who have the talent and ability to become a paid professional athlete are bombarded by countless media entities and fan interactions (especially in the new era of social media outlets like Twitter). They are thrust into positions as role models and public figures whose every move is monitored and scrutinized by the rest of society, leaving people to wonder what it's really like to have an existence so uniquely superior. The simple reason so many top-tier sports professionals are held in such high esteem comes down to the six-, seven-, eight-, and even nine-figure contracts professional athletes sign. Those hefty agreements open doors for even more millions of dollars, which can come in the form of commercial endorsements and appearance fees, not to mention merchandising and licensed products bearing that player's likeness or catch-phrase characteristic. A winner in professional sports becomes a financial boon for himself or herself as well as family members. Among others who benefit are the sports agents who broker the deals and make sure the client is receiving every last penny.

Being a sports agent requires a variety of skills, such as salesmanship, showmanship, tenacity, guile, and cleverness, and also usually a law degree. In many cases, the agent becomes a celebrity as well because of the heightened financial status and position as manager of the careers of so many high-profile athletes. Names such as Leigh Steinberg, Drew Rosenhaus, Scott Boras, and, more recently, rapper Jay-Z have all become familiar to the knowledgeable sports fan for their ability to attract the biggest and brightest athletes. These agents have helped shape sports into the multibillion-dollar worldwide phenomenon that it has become today.

Just over twenty-five years ago, *Sports Illustrated* ran a cover with the phrase "What They Make," regarding Major League Baseball's wage totals from 1987. At the time, the average MLB annual salary was $410,732. The magazine pointed out that the sum was considerably greater than the amounts paid to such historic stars as Ty Cobb and Babe Ruth, who earned $10,000 and $50,000 per year in the years 1911 and 1921, respectively. For some indication on where sports agents have taken the world of big-business athletics, the 2013 MLB average yearly player salary was $3.4 million. In December 2007, the New York Yankees' third baseman, Alex Rodriguez, signed a ten-year, $275-million contract, a financial value that surpasses the *entire* MLB's combined salary total for every player in the league for the 1987 season, which was slightly over $256 million that year.

So how much of an athlete's salary does the agent typically receive? The overall share for a sports agent commonly stands between 4 and 10 percent. In the biggest four sports leagues in the United States, there is no uniformity regarding agent compensation, which illustrates that there is no fixed set of rules, and any deal is ultimately negotiable. Still, one of the concerns is that agents not take too big a cut of their clients' earnings. As a safeguard, the NBA puts a cap on agents' share of the take at 4 percent of an NBA contract. The NFL stipulates that an agent can receive only 3 percent. For MLB and the NHL, there is no set limit on the fee agents may charge, but if, for some reason, it has been uncovered that an agent has demanded an exorbitant fee, the player can take the agent to court on the grounds of conducting business unreasonably. Recent cases hold that a 33.3 percent agent's fee is egregious and worthy of legal examination and potential reduction.

Beyond just a multimillion-dollar player contract, sports agents can additionally collect a predetermined portion of any sponsorship or endorsement deals for their clients—the going rate in those cases is usually 10 percent. The rationale is that the more an agent is allotted percentage-wise, the harder he or she is going to fight for his or her client. Because of this, for many athletes, the thought of conducting a business deal in the sports world would be preposterous without the financial acumen of a licensed sports agent. Still, there have been rare occasions where an athlete has chosen to represent himself, such as Ray Allen during his stint with the Milwaukee Bucks or Tedy Bruschi of the New England Patriots.

Some of the more renowned agencies in all of entertainment and media are also giants of the world of sports. The best known is probably the International Managing Group (IMG), which was founded in 1960 by lawyer Mark McCormack in New York City and now has more than 130 offices in over thirty countries around the world. Current chairman and CEO Michael J. Dolan heads the billion-dollar organization, which now oversees a range of branches, with agents at IMG representing thousands of athletes worldwide. IMG is diverse, with business ventures that extend into the areas of mobile networking, clothes licensing, and team marketing for professional sports franchises, including soccer clubs in the English Premier League and for collegiate athletic programs in the United States. IMG is the model for modern sports media management and a giant in business and finance in the twenty-first century.

Another extremely well-known sports agency is also one of the kings of Hollywood entertainment management: the Creative Artists Agency (CAA). CAA's sports division is presently headed by agent Leon Rose, and oversees more than $700 million in sports player contracts, representing such NBA superstars as Dwyane Wade, Carmelo Anthony, and Chris Paul. In 1996, CAA client Tom Cruise starred in the hit feature film *Jerry Maguire*, a tale about a successful but tormented sports agent who develops a guilty conscience about being someone whose life revolves merely around money, only to spend the rest of the movie fighting for the highest-paying contract for his last remaining client. The irony of that movie illustrates that there really is no other task at hand for a sports agent than bringing in the highest salary in any way possible.

The person responsible for planting the image of movie character Jerry Maguire in the mind of screenwriter and director Cameron Crowe was real-life sports agent Leigh Steinberg. He is to sports agents what Abraham Lincoln is to presidents. He wasn't the first sports agent, but many consider Steinberg to be the best. Born in modest surroundings in 1949 in Los Angeles, California, Steinberg was a go-getter from an early age, being named "Most Likely to Succeed" by his graduating high school class before forming a student government party during his undergraduate career at the University of California at Berkeley. Immediately after earning his bachelor's degree from Berkeley, Steinberg attended and then graduated from the University of California's Hastings College of the Law in 1974, passing the California State Bar soonafter. He went right to work as a sports agent via connections he had made with a fellow student and friend at Cal named Steve Bartkowski, an NFL quarterback from 1975 to 1986. In the nearly four decades since, Steinberg has represented a slew of NFL and MLB players, as well as boxers, Olympic champions, and NBA basketball players. Clients of his have included household names such as Steve Young, Troy Aikman, Ben Roethlisberger,

Dusty Baker, Lennox Lewis, and Oscar de la Hoya. The money associated with contracts brokered by Steinberg easily eclipses $2 billion. The beauty of this for Steinberg is that he's never been punched by a 250-pound heavyweight, sacked by a bloodthirsty defensive end, or beaned by a 97-mile-per-hour fastball.

Another man who would surely be part of the sports agent hall of fame, if it existed, is Scott Boras. His career path to being a player representative was similar to that of Leigh Steinberg, but different in one important respect. Born in 1952 in California's state capital of Sacramento, Boras attended the nearby University of the Pacific, where he was a standout athlete for the Tigers baseball team, hitting .312 as a nineteen-year-old in 1972 and garnering professional interest from many MLB scouts. In 1974, Boras was drafted by the St. Louis Cardinals and sent to their minor-league affiliate in the Florida Gulf Coast League. After playing minor league baseball, Boras found his athletic career cut short by a knee injury in 1977. He went back to the University of the Pacific, where he obtained a pharmacology degree that same year.

Like Leigh Steinberg, Boras was known as a charismatic and intelligent communicator with career aspirations. He was admitted to the McGeorge School of Law in Sacramento, where he earned a law degree in 1982. Though Boras worked in a Chicago-based law firm as a pharmaceutical defense attorney shortly after receiving his law degree, it took only one year for him to negotiate his first big-money sports contract, helping a relatively unknown pitcher named Bill Caudill (who was a close friend of Boras) sign a $7.5 million contract with the Seattle Mariners based on Caudill's one and only notable year during the 1982 baseball season. Scott Boras has never let up since, representing dozens of big-name baseball players over the last three decades, such as Prince Fielder, Stephen Strasburg, Barry Zito, and Matt Holliday. At one point, Scott Boras had a client by the name of Alex Rodriguez, who, in 2000, with Boras' help, penned what was at the time the most lucrative sports contract in history, a $252 million, ten-year deal with the Texas Rangers. Rodriguez has subsequently parted ways with Boras, but that split has done nothing to slow down the man behind billions of dollars of athletic contracts.

A final sports agent who is worthy of closer inspection is Arn Tellem, who currently serves as president of the Wasserman Media Group based in Los Angeles. Tellem is a magnet for NBA and MLB superstars, such as Derrick Rose (five years, $94 million with the Chicago Bulls), Chase Utley (seven years, $85 million with the Philadelphia Phillies), Pau Gasol (three years, $57 million with the Los Angeles Lakers), as well as seven of the top fifteen picks from the 2008 NBA draft. On top of all these lucrative contracts, Arn Tellem has also contributed commentaries and sports columns to major media publications such as the *Huffington Post*, *Sports Illustrated*, and *The New York Times*. There is no telling where the Philadelphia native will display his talents next, but you can bet that it won't be in some sort of unseen inconspicuous manner. Arn Tellem is a giant among giants in the world of sports.

Besides these last three examples, other prominent sports agents include Drew Rosenhaus, whose "Next question!" interview about his client Terrell Owens made him a star of the YouTube age, Tom Condon, who heads the football division of CAA, Mark Steinberg, who represented Tiger Woods on his journey to the heights of professional golf, and, most recently, rapper-turned-agent Jay-Z, who had to sell his ownership share of the NBA's Brooklyn Nets in 2013 in order to kick off his own branch of CAA's sports agency department: Roc Nation Sports. In its short time, Jay-Z's company has signed the likes of professional sports stars Kevin Durant of the NBA's Oklahoma City Thunder and Robinson Cano of the Seattle Mariners, as well as Victor Cruz and Geno Smith of the NFL's New York Giants and Jets, respectively. A shrewd businessman, Jay-Z knows that his stature as a premier player in pop culture affords him the luxury of signing million-dollar athletes who look up to his celebrity. It is an enviable position indeed.

In the second section of this chapter, we take a brief look at the other major source of wealth accumulation for professional athletes and their agents: corporate sponsorships and product endorsements. Anyone who has ever seen a NASCAR race will realize in one second that those aren't cars racing around the track at 190 miles per hour; those are moving billboards that singe a company's logo into the minds of adoring fans. They create an identity for the driver that flat-out would not exist via his or her face alone. I say Tony Stewart, you say Home Depot (and, if you're up on things, you'll now say Office Depot … Stewart loves his depots). I say Dale Earnhardt, Jr., you're thirsty for a Mountain Dew, or thinking about the National Guard. I say Danica Patrick, you shout GoDaddy! Even older race fans know Richard Petty more as the STP pitchman than as the winner of two hundred career NASCAR races. These corporate revenue streams are vital to the pit crews and mechanic teams of every type of professional car racing in the United States and abroad for Le Mans and Formula 1 (aka F1) racing, which dominate the European sports markets. It is literally guaranteed that any car in a professional race will never be devoid of company logos affixed to the driver's jumpsuit and his or her vehicle at all times, because there simply is no sense in wasting space when potential sponsors (and customers) can be gained.

Sponsorships and corporate endorsements now dominate almost every single type of professional sport on the planet. PGA and LPGA golfers constantly don visors and polo shirts bearing the logos of such nonathletic corporate entities as consulting firm KPMG (sponsor of Phil Mickelson) and credit card colossus MasterCard (benefactor of Nick Faldo). As far as sports-related companies are concerned, Nike is ubiquitous in its marketing of golfers like Tiger Woods, and tennis players like Maria Sharapova and Serena Williams. The Oregon-based company is also the official uniform maker for every team in the NFL. Literally, a list of companies and the athletes they sponsor could go on for hundreds of pages. From O. J. Simpson running through an airport for a 1970s Hertz Rent-a-Car commercial to Jim Palmer hawking Jockey underwear in the early 1980s to Bob Uecker's hilarious Miller Lite TV ads, to more contemporary instances such as Michael Phelps pushing Subway sandwiches, or Michael Jordan for Haines, Usain Bolt for Puma, LeBron James for Sprite, McDonalds, Nike, State Farm Insurance, and so forth, keeping track of every endorsement or commercial deal between athletes and their sponsors is not only impossible, it is exhausting.

The main point is that just as much as sports and the media are forever intertwined for each other's benefit, so are athletes and their corporate partners. That is because of the enormous exposure by the media afforded to those lucky and talented individuals. Their high profiles enable the arcs of sports stars to reach fans worldwide. The fans are attracted to products their heroes endorse, and the net result is millions of dollars in product and service sales, with a hefty cut for the athlete. Such is the nature of the business of professional athletics and the circle of life that is sports, sports media, and corporate financial interests.

The dollar values surrounding sports advertising on television have grown steadily during the last few decades, corresponding to the increases in player salaries, endorsement deals, and television broadcast contracts that we have thus far examined in this chapter. In 2011, the total money amount spent by corporate sponsors on TV ads added up to more than $70 billion (bigger than the GDP of more than 120 countries on earth), with athletic-based television advertising covering close to one-sixth of that sum, at $10.9 billion in that one year alone. In the year of 2011, cell phone carrier Verizon was the company spending the most of any business in America, dishing out more than $345 million to showcase its products during sporting events. Coming in second was AT&T, who paid more than $296 million in ad money for TV commercials in and around sports programs, with the top fifty advertisers laying down more than $5.68 billion to have sports fans see their carefully crafted messages. Other substantial money spenders on sports broadcast advertisements include Anheuser-Busch, Ford, Toyota, Chevrolet, Geico, McDonald's, and Nissan, listed in order of most to least ad money disbursed to TV networks for the year 2010.

The paragon of sports advertising on television is the NFL's Super Bowl, which takes place on the first Sunday of February each year. A cultural phenomenon in the United States, the Super Bowl consistently draws nine-figure television audiences, with the Nielsen Company estimating that some 108,400,000 viewers tuned in to watch the Baltimore Ravens defeat the San Francisco 49ers in Super Bowl XLVII on February 3, 2013, the third-largest audience in the game's history. That year, a thirty-second advertising spot cost an average of almost $3.8 million, a record amount of money for the most coveted half-minute on television. The average Super Bowl commercial price did not top $1 million until 1985 and $2 million until 1999. Commercials for the 2014 Super Bowl between the Denver Broncos and the Seattle Seahawks were north of $4,000,000, leaving no room for minor players in this game to win a market share of any number of areas from the United States' annual $15.6 trillion gross domestic product.

These financial amounts are both overwhelming and incredible. The beauty of the Super Bowl is that there are flocks of people who tune in for the game not for the action on the field, but more to see what new and entertaining commercials are being broadcast during time outs. Add to this the fact that there is always a corporate-sponsored halftime show equipped with a brand-name singer (e.g., Pepsi paid $7 million to sponsor Beyoncé's 2013 performance), and the Super Bowl is literally an American institution that people use to time-stamp their lives, absorbing pop culture as it is displayed in full force on the world's biggest stage: a television screen.

Elsewhere, Internet advertising is a multibillion-dollar business in the current decade of the 2010s, growing to unseen levels as more people take to using smartphones and handheld computer tablets when not sitting down in front of their laptops. In 2012, online ad revenue surpassed print media (i.e., newspapers and magazines) for the first time in history, with Internet commercials and banner advertisements yielding websites $39.5 billion, versus $33.8 billion for the diminished sector using paper instead of megabytes. By 2016, the ratio is expected to be even more skewed toward Internet revenue for business ads, with the values predicted at $62 billion to $32.3 billion in favor of cyberspace. While it is difficult to determine the precise values of which advertising expenditures are going specifically to sports-related websites (because of the fact that the corporate web hosts mix their numbers into the overall revenue intake disclosed to the public), Internet advertising overall rose 15 percent in 2012 from the previous year, beginning a trend that experts predict will last for quite some time. Surely sports are driving this tendency toward advertising on the Internet as bandwidth increases and high-speed wireless connections allow for live events to be streamed to a computer, phone, or tablet in no less quality than one would enjoy at home on a large HDTV.

To conclude, playing games for fun is something that takes place throughout the world, but competing for the highest stakes possible helps authenticate the social value of sports in our world. Athletics is a major piece of the fiscal puzzle that drives not only local and regional communities, but entire sectors of the world's economies. As the future of sports media approaches, these business deals will only get larger, reaching loftier peaks as populations grow and technology spreads the love of sports throughout the ever-shrinking world in which we live. No matter where top-level sports are headed, huge sums of money will certainly follow close behind. The goal is to make a profit from investments in the players and media sources that exhibit the talents and competitive matchups that fans long for on a daily basis throughout the year. There seems to be no end in sight.

11

Sports Films Throughout the Ages

What is art? Is it even a question that can be answered? One approach to defining art is to see it as the search for truth. It's not a truth in the way that two plus two equals four. It is a truth of the body and soul, wherein human beings never need to question that a certain sentiment is honest and true. A chord is struck within the emotional palate of the reader or viewer, and the message sent from the artist is received and remembered forever. Such is the case with so many of the wonderful sports films that cinematic artists have created during the past one hundred years in the United States.

The field of sports in general is predisposed to creating a visceral emotional response in the people who witness the real-world struggles and tales of triumph. They are the key ingredients to any unforgettable athletic legend. The universal emotions of being the underdog, of vying to break out and show the world that we *are* good enough, despite the odds, and that we have what it takes to demonstrate honor and integrity, resonate with humans. That is why so many sports films are collaborative works of art. The compelling stories behind them drive everyone associated with a project (the writers, directors, and actors) into being the best they can be, because they all feel that truth as well.

Chronologically speaking, one of the very first feature-length sports movies made in America was *Heading Home*, a fifty-five-minute silent film that was released in 1920 starring New York Yankee baseball legend Babe Ruth, who played a fictionalized version of himself as a young man rising from meager roots to become the most beloved athletic hero on the planet. Perhaps because the story was not a true biography of The Babe, it might seem that the real Sultan of Swat came from prosperous beginnings. In actuality, Ruth spent most of his childhood in reformatories in and around Baltimore, Maryland, a narrative no less compelling than the *Heading Home* plot. Nonetheless, Hollywood saw fit to dress things up, a characteristic of the movie industry that has existed since the very start.

The first "talkie" film about sports to win critical acclaim was 1931's *The Champ*, which starred Wallace Beery as the title character, Andy "Champ" Purcell, an alcoholic boxer at the end of his career vying to regain some semblance of dignity for his eight-year-old son Dink. The movie plays out the compelling character arc of a man putting his life back together to fight in one final big bout, winning with every last ounce of strength left in his body, only to collapse and die in the film's final scene. Champ's son sees his father as someone with great honor and courage, so the man is redeemed by his heroic willingness to risk everything to restore his good name. The film was nominated for four Oscars at the 1932 Academy Awards in Los Angeles, including Best Picture and Best Director for King Vidor, with Beery taking home Best Actor for his inspirational and timeless role, one that would be emulated numerous times in future boxing-themed films. As one final note of worth regarding *The Champ*, the film won the 1932 Academy Award for Best Screenplay for the script penned by Frances Marion, a historically significant woman who served as a combat correspondent during World War I before moving on to sports journalism and screenwriting. Marion is often considered to be the best female screenwriter of the twentieth century. She won another Oscar for Best Screenplay for 1930's *The Big House*, and she scripted more than a dozen more feature films during her prosperous career.

Another early sports film with an everlasting legacy is *Knute Rockne, All-American*, which appeared in theaters in 1940. The biographical movie featured Pat O'Brien as the iconic football player and coach of Notre Dame, with future president Ronald Reagan playing George Gipp, the real-life All-American halfback for the Fighting Irish who died of strep throat in 1920 at the age of twenty-five. The film showcased the life and times of Rockne, one of college football's historic champions, as both player and then head coach. He ran the Notre Dame football team from 1918 to 1930, winning four National Championships and pioneering the use of the forward pass in football, differentiating the sport from rugby and giving American football the unique identity it still exhibits today. The film's most famous quote, spoken by Rockne to inspire his team, put the words "win one for the Gipper" into the American lexicon. It also gave Reagan a nice campaign slogan to use several years down the line on his road to the White House.

The 1942 classic that solidified Gary Cooper's status as one of Hollywood's all-time legends was *The Pride of the Yankees*, a heavy-hearted tale of baseball ironman Lou Gehrig, who died just one year prior to the film's release. The movie chronicles Gehrig's rise to prominence as a major leaguer, up to the point of his "Luckiest Man on the Face of the Earth" speech, which he gave at Yankee Stadium shortly after acquiring the debilitating motor neuron disease amyotrophic lateral sclerosis (ALS) in 1938. ALS, also known as Lou Gehrig's disease, was the only thing that could halt Gehrig's consecutive-game streak at 2,130 starts (a mark bettered only by the Baltimore Orioles' Cal Ripken, Jr., in 1995). It is nearly impossible for any baseball fan to watch *The Pride of the Yankees* and not need a box of tissues and a hug from a friend. The film, rightfully so, was honored with eleven nominations at the 1943 Academy Awards, winning an Oscar for Best Film Editing.

Switching away from team sports, 1944's *National Velvet* showcased the poignant story of a twelve-year-old girl named Velvet, played by a precocious Elizabeth Taylor in her first Hollywood starring role. In the movie, Velvet wins an unruly, unwanted horse in a raffle and trains it for England's Grand National steeplechase. Also in a lead role alongside Taylor was the popular Mickey Rooney in the part of Mi, a farmhand who aids Velvet in her quest to make her horse a champion. The film features a memorable final race where Velvet takes the reins, unbeknownst to her family and the on-looking crowd, showing people that girls can ride and succeed just as well as the boys. The film received much acclaim at the time, and was nominated for five Oscars at the 1946 Academy Awards, winning two.

A famous and extremely well-known boxing film from 1962 starred Anthony Quinn as the lead character Louis "Mountain" Rivera in *Requiem for a Heavyweight*. Much in the same boxing vein as *The Champ*, *Requiem for a Heavyweight* gives the account of a boxer whose career is at its end. Quinn's portrayal of the punch-drunk, brain-damaged boxer was both moving and memorable. Jackie Gleason costars as Rivera's manager, unscrupulously pushing the fighter into more bouts despite the clear medical risks, because of his own need to settle gambling debts with the mob. The film includes a cameo appearance in an opening scene by Muhammad Ali (billed under his birth name, Cassius Clay), who fights Rivera and nearly knocks the life out of him. The movie's ending involves a twist where Mountain agrees to work as a professional wrestler to pay off his manager's debt obligations. The film cemented Quinn's legacy as one of Hollywood's great actors.

A football film that stands as one of the most honest depictions of lost friendship ever made is 1971's *Brian's Song*, which first aired on TV on the ABC network. Despite being a made-for-TV movie, it is regarded as a masterpiece of sports on any screen, telling the heartbreaking saga of Brian Piccolo and his best friend and teammate Gayle Sayers, played by James Caan and Billy Dee Williams, respectively. *Brian's Song* recounts the years in which Piccolo and Sayers were roommates for the Chicago Bears in the mid- to late 1960s, a rarity in the racially segregated times. In the 1969 NFL season, Piccolo was diagnosed with a quickly spreading terminal cancer, and Sayers was there with his friend until June 1970, when Piccolo died at twenty-six years of age. The juxtaposition of on-the-field gladiator versus a devastating disease that affects even the mightiest of humans put the irrepressible nature of cancer into perspective. The film showed the tenderness inside all of us that springs forth when we know someone's time on Earth is limited. Brian Piccolo was a fighter until the end, and his story can inspire anyone who watches *Brian's Song* to want to live every moment to the fullest.

Getting back to boxing, one would be hard-pressed to find a person who has never heard of the 1976 film *Rocky*, which won Best Picture at the 1977 Academy Awards, along with two other Oscars out of its ten total nominations. It was directed by John Avildsen and starred Sylvester Stallone (who also wrote the script) in his breakout performance as the "Italian Stallion" Rocky Balboa. *Rocky* is the fictional tale of a Philadelphia bruiser who gets a one-in-a-million chance at the title against heavyweight champion Apollo Creed, played Carl Weathers. The movie succeeds not because of its oft-clichéd theme of underdog who can rise to glory in one instant, but because of the honest tone of overcoming life's hardships while loving and respecting those who mean the most. Both Rocky and his girlfriend Adrian (played by Talia Shire) are dismissed as being nobodies whose fates are destined for obscurity, but the story illustrates the complex nature of every person. It shows that we all have unique characteristics that can make our lives meaningful, especially when we find someone we love. In the film's epic final sequence, Rocky is raised to monumental heights by standing in the ring toe to toe with Apollo Creed and not backing down. The outcome of the fight means little when so much has already been accomplished.

A critically acclaimed film that dealt with the rarely-covered sporting topic of bicycle racing was 1979's *Breaking Away*, starring Dennis Christopher and Dennis Quaid as recent high school graduates from the Indiana University town of Bloomington. The story centers on the struggles of racing enthusiast Dave Stoller, played by Christopher, who comes from a working-class family like the rest of his biking buddies. Dave and his friends do not fit in with the more affluent IU students especially when it comes to gaining respect as bike racers at the college, scene of the prestigious annual "Little 500" bicycle competition, a fifty-mile race on a university track. Although Dave isn't enrolled at IU, he is invited to compete in the 500 by the university president after a run-in with some bullying students. In the end, Dave and his friends are able to fight for well-warranted respect while competing for glory. The race lets the protagonist patch things up with his father and develop the courage necessary to move on toward greater things in his life. *Breaking Away* was honored with five Academy Award nominations, taking home Best Original Screenplay for Indiana University graduate Steve Tesich at the 1980 Oscars.

In terms of films that captured the spirit of an entire nation, Great Britain's *Chariots of Fire*, which was released in 1981, told the touching tale of two runners en route to the 1924 Summer Olympics held in Paris. The movie was centered in religious sanctity, recounting the competitive relationship between a devout Scottish Christian named Eric Liddell and an English Jew named Harold Abrahams, Cambridge University classmates in 1919. While both men were above and beyond their peers skill-wise, both faced spiritual peril: Liddell could not compete on Sundays, and Abrahams was the victim of anti-Semitism at Cambridge. Each had his chances of success affected because of religion. By the time the movie reaches the gold medal races in the Olympic Games, audiences have been captivated by the beautiful cinematography, compelling screenplay, and hypnotic theme song by Greek composer Vangelis, which garnered him an Oscar for Best Song at the 1982 Academy Awards. *Chariots of Fire* also won three other Oscars that year, including Best Picture, along with Best Costume Design and Best Original Screenplay for writer Colin Welland.

A classic baseball film that was nominated four times at the 1985 Academy Awards was 1984's *The Natural*, an adapted novel that featured Robert Redford as the mysterious slugger Roy Hobbs, who rose to fame during the 1939 MLB season as an aged thirty-five-year-old outfielder. The movie costarred Glenn Close as Hobbs' childhood sweetheart who rekindles his love for life, and screen great Robert Duvall as a sportswriter who suspects something is amiss about the rapid ascension of the unknown baseball player taking the world by storm. The film features Redford's character Hobbs pulling off divine feats on the playing field (such as knocking the cover off a baseball with a mighty swing or pitching a ball past a representation of Babe Ruth). Fans and the media were mesmerized in a way that happens over and over again today when the public yearns for the next big thing, whether it be a rising young star or an out-of-nowhere success story. The film's finale gives sports movie fans a sight to remember, with Hobbs smashing a pitch into the lights, exploding the bulbs in a moment of wonder as the story reaches its tender conclusion with the ballplayer putting his life back into full order. Truly, *The Natural* contains all the best qualities of a film that embodies fighting for redemption against all odds and reaching a state of honest fulfillment because of persistence and solid integrity.

Another beloved sports movie from 1984 tells the coming-of-age saga of Daniel LaRusso, aka *The Karate Kid*, a teenage Jersey boy who travels to the Los Angeles area's San Fernando Valley with his mother, who is seeking a fresh start to their lives. Ralph Macchio won the hearts of filmgoers with his vulnerable depiction of the new kid trying to fit in, only to be bullied by Johnny Lawrence (played by William Zabka) and his evil Cobra Kai cronies. Daniel's fate as a punching bag seems secured until he is taken under the wing by his apartment building's Japanese maintenance man and secret karate master, Mr. Miyagi. Miyagi became a character for the ages, thanks to the Oscar-nominated craftsmanship from actor Pat Morita. Whether or not people love seeing Johnny sweep the leg to try to put Daniel in a body bag, nothing beats a perfect crane kick to the chin to make you want to rise from your seat and cheer for a newfound hero discovering that he has what it takes thanks to his dedication, hard work, and adherence to the lessons of a wise and honorable teacher.

Next comes a sports picture so esteemed that of the one hundred best sports films of all time, many rate this movie at the top of the list. For anyone who has ever traveled through the Midwest on a beautiful autumn evening, 1986's *Hoosiers* conjures up memories of high school gymnasiums filled with the delicious smell of fresh popcorn and the gentle squeak of high-top shoes on the wooden basketball floor. The story gives a loosely based account of the 1954 Milan High School boys' team, which, despite incalculable odds, won the Indiana State Championship against a school with an enrollment ten times greater than the mere 161 students from the tiny town. *Hoosiers* features Gene Hackman in the role of Coach Norman Dale and Dennis Hopper as his alcoholic but inspirational assistant, Shooter, who takes command of the team in one key moment of the movie, orchestrating a game-winning bucket on a clever play. Hopper's portrayal of the tormented father earned him an Oscar nomination for Best Supporting Actor at the 1987 Academy Awards. The film was stocked with unknown performers playing utterly authentic young basketball players who believed in one another and weren't afraid to succeed in the face of the highest stakes possible versus extremely intimidating opponents. If any high school coach ever mentions a play called the "Picket Fence," you can believe that he or she is a big fan of this celebrated movie classic.

Rounding out our look at sports movies from the 1980s comes the cherished 1989 film *Field of Dreams*, starring Kevin Costner in his second hit baseball-themed feature in as many years (he also starred in 1988's *Bull Durham* as a catcher named Crash Davis, who must mentor an egotistical young pitcher for a North Carolina minor league team). In *Field of Dreams*, Costner plays Ray Kinsella, who lives as a struggling farmer with his wife and adolescent daughter in rural Iowa. One day, Ray hears a whispering voice in the empty corn fields telling him, "If you build it, he will come." Seemingly possessed by the absurd notion of cutting down his crops to construct a full-scale baseball field in the middle of nowhere, Kinsella does exactly this despite the pleas of his brother-in-law, who warns of an oncoming foreclosure to the farm. Upon construction of the field, long-dead players from the humiliated 1919 Chicago White Sox team that threw the World Series begin showing up in Ray's field, playing as the unblemished young men they once were, giving Ray a sense of vindication about his risky choice. The film grabs the hearts of viewers when the story reveals that the reason for the voices among the corn stalks was to assist various people in reconciliations with their pasts. The most important patch-up is between Ray and his estranged father, with whom he had had a falling out many years earlier. As the film ends, hundreds of cars wait lined up to see Ray's magical field of dreams, reminding people that staying true to one's convictions with integrity can result in a mystical twist of fate anywhere on Earth.

An inspiring 1993 film about a real-life Notre Dame football player is *Rudy*, which stars Sean Astin as the diminutive title character, Daniel "Rudy" Ruettiger, who grew up with the obsession of playing for the renowned Fighting Irish. In spite of mind-numbing odds keeping the young man from being a Division I college football player (such as his height of just 5′6″, his dyslexia, and the fact that he wasn't accepted as a student at Notre Dame), Rudy remained persistent, working for free as a groundskeeper at the school's stadium and meeting with a tutor to become worthy of admission to the university. Because of his insistence on achieving his lifelong goal and resistance to surrendering his dream, Rudy is given an opportunity to play for Notre Dame in a 1976 game, where he became part of the school's historic tradition, recording a sack before being carried off the field as a hero by his admiring teammates.

One film masterpiece that was shockingly overlooked by the Academy Award nominating committee was 1994's *Hoop Dreams*, a stunning sports documentary that involved more than five years of filming of the formative times of two inner-city Chicago basketball players, William Gates and Arthur Agee. Directed by Steve James, the movie shows every gripping moment of hope and despair for the two young boys who are recruited as eighth graders to attend the private and predominantly white, Catholic St. Joseph High School in the Chicago suburbs. The school was home to NCAA and NBA legend Isiah Thomas, who graduated in 1979. Set against the backdrop of Michael Jordan's Chicago Bulls glory years, *Hoop Dreams* documents the unfair burden placed on the shoulders of the two players, whose families are depending on them to conquer incredibly insurmountable odds to become basketball stars. As a documentary, this film is exempt from Hollywood's golden luster and fictional storybook endings, and the physical and emotional struggles besetting the boys prove that nothing in life comes easy, but perseverance can prevail. Any basketball fan who has not seen this film should put this spectacular work of art at the top of his or her to-do list.

Moving into the twenty-first century, we have seen nothing but an increase in the number of memorable sports films produced by the world's biggest movie studios. In terms of football, there is *Remember the Titans* from 2000, starring Denzel Washington; *Friday Night Lights* from 2004, with Billy Bob Thornton; 2006's *We Are Marshall,* featuring Matthew McConaughey; and *Invincible*, also from 2006, with Mark Wahlberg. Two popular horseracing films from recent years based on real events are *Seabiscuit*, which was released in 2003 and starred Tobey Maguire as a fearless jockey, and *Secretariat*, which hit theaters in 2010 and featured Diane Lane. One soccer movie produced by a British studio in 2002 was *Bend It Like Beckham*, a stirring family drama that starred Keira Knightley. The film has motivated girls from all over the world to try their best to achieve goal-scoring glory. A film from 2004 that chronicled the phenomenal run by the U.S. Men's Hockey Team to a gold medal in the 1980 Winter Olympics was *Miracle*. The movie gave Kurt Russell top billing as Coach Herb Brooks, the man who made his team believe that although they were unknown and undersized, they still had the heart to defeat the mighty Soviets and prove their worth as the world's best hockey team. Finally, there was the basketball movie *Glory Road* from 2006, which presented the true saga of the 1966 Texas Western University men's team (the school is now called UTEP, or the University of Texas at El Paso). The team started five African American players and was the first squad of that nature to win the NCAA tournament, defeating the University of Kentucky in the championship game, along with Wildcat coach Adolph Rupp, who refused to ever consider allowing a black player on any of his teams. There is absolutely no doubt that more sports films will be coming in the near future to a theater near you, especially as the real world of athletics keeps turning out compelling stories deserving of being celebrated on the silver screen.

Other subgenres of sports films include the biographical picture (or biopic), a type of movie that follows a particular athlete from his or her early days along the path to the top of the profession, involving the prominent instances of strife and peril that the person overcame while achieving athletic glory. One example of these films was *Ali* from 2001, starring Will Smith as the greatest boxer of all time in a role that earned him his first career Oscar nomination. Another was 2013's compelling movie *42*, about Brooklyn Dodgers superstar Jackie Robinson, who broke the MLB color barrier in 1947. A 1994 baseball film that starred Tommy Lee Jones and earned him a Best Actor Academy Award nomination for his role as the notoriously vile, record-setting hitter Ty Cobb is a film expectedly named *Cobb*. The 1951 biopic *Jim Thorpe, All-American* featured Burt Lancaster in the lead role as one of the most versatile athletes in American history, displaying Thorpe's prominent career as a college football star at the Carlisle Indian Industrial School. There, he singlehandedly led his team to the 1912 National Championship.

The final subgenre of sports movies is the sports comedy, of which there have been several unforgettable classics. Some of these films include 1980's *Caddyshack*, a riotous affair about a young golf caddy trying to earn a scholarship to college via a tournament at a snobby country club. The film featured comic geniuses such as Rodney Dangerfield, Chevy Chase, and Bill Murray in an unforgettably hilarious role as the inappropriate greens keeper Carl Spackler, who steals every scene in which he appears. Another comedy classic is 1976's *Bad News Bears,* about a rag-tag group of little league baseball players whose team would be lucky to win one game, let alone play for the championship. The film features Walter Matthau as the alcoholic manager and Tatum O'Neil as the sharp-tongued pitcher who proves that a headstrong girl can hold her own on and off the field. One year later, in 1977, a hockey film named *Slap Shot* appeared at the box office, featuring Paul Newman and three peculiar, glasses-wearing brothers named Jeff, Steve, and Jack Hanson. That film is virtually required viewing in hockey-crazed Canada. In 1989, a star-studded film about baseball called *Major League* became a major hit that year, thanks to memorable characters such as Willie "Mays" Hayes, played by Wesley Snipes, and ex-convict Ricky Vaughn, in a career-turning role for Charlie Sheen. The film also features Bob Uecker as a boozing radio broadcaster for the fictional Cleveland Indians team that can't seem to do anything right at first, even if they're "juuuuust a bit outside." These movies prove that sports has so many entertaining features that lend themselves perfectly to the medium of film, especially because of the colorful characters on the field who bring so much to the table beyond their amazing physical talents.

All apologies for not detailing other great sports films, such as 1979's *North Dallas Forty* (based on a book by Michigan State University graduate Peter Gent), 1988's *Eight Men Out*, 1980's *Raging Bull*, 1999's *The Hurricane*, 1961's *The Hustler*, 1986's *The Color of Money*, and 2009's *Invictus* and *The Blind Side*, along with the other dozens of athletically themed movies from the past one hundred years. Truly, the topic of sports films in general could start a discussion on par with any other sports talk debate over which team was the best across different eras or what player deserves to be considered the greatest of all time. These films have such staying power in the hearts and minds of the viewing public because of the truthful honesty of their stories and inspirational tales of achievement that exemplify the finest human traits—overcoming obstacles and striving to be the best one can be. This is why the movies discussed in this chapter are clear works of art, and why they will continue to be watched and enjoyed by audiences for the next one hundred years and beyond.

12

The Future of Sports Media

The future is now! These are words that rang out in the post–World War II era of the 1950s, when technological expansion brought consumer products like the television set to households throughout the United States. Then came the early 1980s and the advent of the desktop computer, thanks to Steve Wozniak and Steve Jobs at Apple, along with Bill Gates and his DOS operating system. The next step was to link the computer and word processor to the World Wide Web, allowing people to communicate and share ideas in a manner that knocked down physical barriers. Now we can literally carry in the palms of our hands gadgets that are thousands of times faster and exponentially more powerful than any computer available as recently as the 1990s.

The beauty of technological innovation is that it never ends—it will continue to amaze as people discover solutions to problems they never imagined. In a world where humans desire constant communication with others, like sharing information about themselves, other people, and circumstances around them, the role of the media has never been more important. This begs the question: what is media? The late scholar Marshall McLuhan suggested that media is and will always be an extension of the human body. The media quickens the capability to perform duties that were at one time impossible but now can be completed almost instantaneously in some cases, all thanks to imagination and clever ingenuity. As such, the car is a type of media, and so is the telephone, as is the Internet, as are social web services such as Facebook and Twitter. Anything that

increases the capacity to communicate with others and accomplish tasks faster can be considered media. The future of media will surely hold more surprises as ideas are connected in new ways like never before.

The twenty-first century has seen the arrival of the brave new world of technological convergence. It is fueled by faster-working hardware and the Internet, allowing many seemingly different types of media to work in harmony to perform similar tasks. Phones from a variety of companies are now able to take photographs, record audio, transmit video in live streams, access websites, send text messages, play music, access maps, and delve into Smithsonian-sized libraries of books. At the same time, the devices can access newsfeeds, magazines, journal articles, movie clips, pictures, recipes, and sports scores. They can do all of this while chiming a preset alarm clock notification with accompanying notated reminders. This convergent technology facilitates the orderly and noiseless transmission of information from sender to receiver, known as the process of communication. The boundaries of this expansion are limitless, and information can now be transferred immediately on an infinite scale. Only a few years ago, people were concerned with backing up mere megabytes of information on a zip disk. We now operate in gigabytes and terabytes, with petabytes surely on the way to the average computer user in the near future. Anyone reading this should note the date of publication and realize that the word *exabyte* isn't in the vernacular at this point in time but will be in a decade, if not sooner. There is no precise way to know how quickly things are going to evolve.

The world *has* evolved at a more noticeably rapid pace, with even average tech users frequently operating several computer-based devices in a day, if not at the same time. Often the smartphone, laptop and television are all within direct eyesight. The central question for our discussion now becomes: what does this all have to do with sports? For the answer, let's take a look at Twitter.

Founded in March 2006 by web developer Jack Dorsey, based in San Francisco, Twitter is a combination of text messaging and the search-based functionality of websites such as Google or Yahoo. Users are able to create and control their own accounts, constructing and disseminating messages that are limited to 140 characters per tweet. The beauty of Twitter (and the bane to some) is that once a tweet has been sent, it becomes openly searchable by anyone who possesses the freely downloadable Twitter app or anyone else on a web browser who visits search.twitter.com. Tweets can be deleted, but once the toothpaste is out of the tube, it's never going back in. Tweets remain available thanks to the ability of anyone to access Twitter backlogs, or from one single person taking a screen capture of the tweet prior to its removal (screen captures of deleted tweets are one of the more popular items on the Internet).

It took Twitter a few years to be fully embraced by people throughout the world, but by 2012, there were more than five hundred million registered Twitter accounts total, and by 2013, people were providing more than 340 million tweets per day, with more than 1.6 billion searches of tweets occurring every twenty-four hours. Twitter had arrived as a major player in all media once television mainstays such as ESPN and CNN began the common practice of showing tweets on the screen during broadcasts, illustrating the interconnected nature of social media and broadcasting. The beauty of nearly all of these tweets is that the places and people from whom these bits of opinion are coming are of no matter. Of consequence is that someone out there is voicing a viewpoint that may be similar or different from the one you yourself are holding. It creates an internal monologue sparked by outside sources, which is nothing new, but in the case of Twitter, people can jump online or onto their app, search the tweet, and reply directly over the public channel via what is known as a re-tweet. The simplicity of the interpersonal communication is the genius of its structure, which is almost always the case for significant modernization.

In conjunction with this ease of using the Twitter interface to type up and send along information, it allows a way for anyone to create and maintain personal accounts. A sports fan can now interact directly with an athletic celebrity, just as a newspaper reader can mingle with a sportswriter, and so forth. Does this mean that everyone on Twitter is on equal footing? Of course not, and we will examine this characteristic right now.

One of the most alluring aspects of the service is the prominent position on people's accounts of the number of "followers"—those who subscribe directly to others as the individuals disseminate information. There is much social capital to be gained by accruing the greatest number of followers possible. This tends to give credibility to the statements, simply because so many others are ostensibly interested in hearing them. This is nothing new in the world of social networking, as websites such as MySpace and Facebook have proven in the case of number of friends. But with MySpace and Facebook, there is a point where having "too many" friends becomes unmanageable. With such a network it is too hard to maintain an aura of popularity. How can anyone realistically manage that many real-life friendships? With Twitter, the sky is the limit, because an account holder is sharing only thoughts, and if 100,000 people have signed up to see those standpoints, it must be because they hold so much weight. This is why the phrase "follow me on Twitter" can ring hollow, because it illuminates an inherent need for humans to feel popular via some sort of quantified tally.

For the record, Canadian wunderkind Justin Bieber currently leads the way with the most Twitter followers on Earth, with more than forty-three million accounts signed up to follow the superstar's celebrity status updates and bits of wisdom. Coming in second with more than forty-one million followers is singer Katy Perry, with Lady Gaga trailing in third place with thirty-nine million devoted followers. In terms of sports celebrities and those working in sports media, there are quite a few individuals with hordes of followers as well. In 2013, the most popular athlete in the Twittersphere was LeBron James (or @KingJames), with nearly 10 million followers, ranking him number 62 on the twitaholic.com rankings (for the record, President Barack Obama was fourth in the list, with more than thirty-five million followers). That is *not* to say that there aren't hundreds of thousands of athletes and sportswriters amassing even greater numbers of followers. The NBA, as an organization, is the second-highest sports Twitter account, with nearly eight million followers, which places it eighty-seventh on the list. ESPN comes in at ninety-ninth, with nearly seven million Twitter followers.

The main point is that every single sports person of any noteworthy public status—and those who desire to be—can almost be guaranteed to have a regularly maintained Twitter account. Every NFL player, NBA player, MLB player, NHL player, NCAA football or basketball player, and professional sportswriter or devoted sports blogger tweets frequently. A random sampling of some familiar names in sports reveals the following statistics on the number of Twitter followers for each: Jay Bilas (from ESPN College Basketball)—564,000 followers, Mark Cuban (billionaire owner of the NBA's Dallas Mavericks)—1.8 million, Kevin Durant (NBA star of the Oklahoma City Thunder)—4.7 million, Floyd Mayweather, Jr. (five-division world champion boxer)—4 million, Bubba Watson (PGA golfing champion)—983,000, and Dan Wetzel (Yahoo! Sports columnist)—162,000. The average major newspaper or web-based sportswriter can easily garner more than ten thousand followers because of local interest these days. There truly are no rules to the game, and the old adage remains that any publicity is good publicity.

The most intriguing (and at the same time frightening) feature of Twitter lies in its ability to allow people to disseminate unfiltered information to the public without any deliberation. It is possible to send out raw and unedited nuggets of information that can provide a glimpse into the true thoughts of the person behind the tweet. In the past, sports franchises and organizations could keep a cap on most of the gossip and rumors swirling about within their establishments, but in this era, athletes and their friends and family members only need to access their Twitter accounts to put previously guarded secrets out into the open. Once revealed, the information cannot be retracted. It is impossible to un-ring a bell.

Several infamous examples of Twitter helping to "spill the beans" about some athletes' opinions or secrets have included ex–Pittsburgh Steelers running back Rashard Mendenhall, who in 2011 questioned why people were celebrating Osama bin Laden's death. In his view via several tweets, 9/11 was a conspiracy that should be reexamined. Those messages cost him millions of dollars in lost endorsement contracts because of his controversial stance. Another NFL player who landed in hot water was ex–Kansas City Chiefs running back Larry Johnson, who made two gay slurs on his Twitter account in 2009, costing him $213,000 in salary because of the one-game suspension levied against him.

In regard to sports transaction secrets and the transparency of social media, there was the case of NBA All-Star center Dwight Howard, who jumped the gun of his team's official announcement in June 2013. He tweeted the news one full week prior to the national press conference unveiling the blockbuster deal, notifying the public in one fell swoop that he would be signing a new contract with the Houston Rockets rather than re-sign with the Los Angeles Lakers. Talk about a spoiler alert. Another similar example involved NBA player Kevin Love of the Minnesota Timberwolves, who tweeted that his head coach Kevin McHale was not returning to the team the next season. That undercut the official announcement that the franchise wanted to manage so that they could have found a new replacement without it appearing like they weren't in control of the team's public relations.

There are numerous other examples of players speaking too candidly about their opinions of fans, or family members sharing secrets, all of which have many real-life consequences. For the most part, mouthing off via Twitter ends up costing players money. Truly, it is better to keep one's mouth shut, which is perhaps why there is such a fascination with Twitter, because it enables the least shrewd communicators to have a direct pipeline to the masses.

More important than loose lips that reveal errors in judgment, the effect of Twitter means that speculation and rumor-based gossip can spread like wildfire. It is reminiscent of the popular telephone game played by grade-school children, where the final message sounds nothing like the original one. Subsequently, for reporters and fans alike, everything must be taken with a grain of salt and verified in as many different ways possible. Even then, things aren't always what they seem. This "what if?" factor has singlehandedly pushed college football and basketball recruiting into a never-before-seen level of prominence. As a result, websites such as Rivals.com and Scout.com have sold for millions of dollars ($100 million for Rivals, $50 million for Scout) to media conglomerates Yahoo! and Fox Sports, respectively. These days, any local sportswriter or amateur sports enthusiast can circulate the news about a certain collegiate head coach attending a high school game to witness a highly touted recruit, hatching conjecture and guesswork about the player's possible future destination. Fans at home read the tweets, post to chat forums, and constantly check for updates about these recruits. That activity fuels advertising revenue for the websites, which in turn drives the urge for the media to break stories on the next big decision for an important player. It is a cycle that will most likely continue to help grow the world of recruiting news websites as the current decade progresses.

The expansion of technology has enabled messages to be transferred on an infinite scale to anyone who tunes in to whichever major branches of sports media he or she chooses to consume. If an occurrence involves a bit of new information about something worthwhile, it will undoubtedly make its way to the major hubs of sports reporting in a matter of minutes (or seconds). This raises many of the ethical questions discussed in chapter 8. It also points out that there is a shrinking amount of privacy afforded to those who choose to inhabit the public sphere—almost the entire sector of athletics and sports media. What the future specifically holds will always contain some amount of uncertainty, but there is an overwhelming chance that we are going to continue in the direction that the Internet and smartphone technology have taken us so far in the twenty-first century. It is toward a world characterized by more knowledge, less secrets, and a thirst for attention from anyone seeking to make a name in the world of sports and sports media.

References

Chap. 1—History of Sports Part I: Ancient History & Chap. 2—History of Sports Part II: Sports Media

Americas Cup Event Authority LLC. "A Journey through History/America's Cup." Accessed October 8, 2012. http://www.americascup.com/en/about/history.

American Football Coaches Association . "Top 25 Coaches' Poll." Accessed September 21, 2012. https://www.afca.com/article/article.php?id=USAPOLL_INTRO.

Baran, Stanley J. "Sports and Television." *The Museum of Broadcast Communications*. Accessed September 25, 2012. http://www.museum.tv/eotvsection.php?entrycode=sportsandte.

Barbor, Phil. "Newspaper History." *Phil Barber's Historic Newspaper Shop*. Accessed September 15, 2012. http://www.historicpages.com/nprhist.htm.

Brasch, R. *How Did Sports Begin?* Hong Kong, China: Peninsula Press, 1972.

The British Museum. "Royal Tombs of Ur." Accessed September 12, 2012. http://www.mesopotamia.co.uk/tombs/challenge/cha_set.html.

Cuddon, J.A. *The International Dictionary of Sports and Games*. New York: Schocken Books, 1980.

Encyclopedia Britannica Online. "Battle of Marathon (Greek History)." Accessed September 10, 2012. http://www.britannica.com/EBchecked/topic/363914/Battle-of-Marathon.

Encyclopedia Britannica Online. "Olympic Games." Accessed September 19, 2012. http://www.britannica.com/EBchecked/topic/428005/Olympic-Games.

Encyclopedia Britannica Online. "Pankration." Accessed September 14, 2012. http://www.britannica.com/EBchecked/topic/440968/pankration.

Encyclopedia Britannica Online. "Sports." Accessed September 9, 2012. http://www.britannica.com/EBchecked/topic/561041/sports.

ESPN.com. "ABC Sports – Wide World of Sports." Accessed October 9, 2012. http://espn.go.com/abcsports/wwos/milestones/1990s.html.

ESPN.com. "Hall of Fame manager Sparky Anderson dies." Accessed September 21, 2012. http://sports.espn.go.com/mlb/news/story?id=5764168.

ESPN.com. "Monday Night Football – History of ABC's Monday Night Football." Accessed October 8, 2012. http://espn.go.com/abcsports/mnf/s/2003/0115/1493105.html.

Everest News. "Everest Facts." Accessed September 14, 2012. http://www.everestnews.com/everest1.htm.

FIFA.com. "History of Football." Accessed September 9, 2012.http://www.fifa.com/classicfootball/history/index.html.

The Football Network. "The Japanese and Kemari." Accessed October 3, 2012. http://www.footballnetwork.org/dev/historyoffootball/history2.asp.

Fuller, Linda K. *Sportscasters/Sportscasting: Principles and Practices*. New York, New York: Routledge, 2008.

Gems, Gerald R., and Gertrud Pfister. *Understanding American Sports*. London: Routledge, 2009.

Greene, Bob. "Why baseball managers wear uniforms." *CNN.com*. Accessed September 25, 2012. http://www.cnn.com/2011/10/23/opinion/greene-baseball-manager-uniforms/index.html.

Harris, H.A. *Sport in Greece and Rome*. Ithaca, New York: Cornell University Press, 1972.

Historyworld.net. "History of Sports and Games." Accessed September 10, 2012. http://www.historyworld.net/wrldhis/PlainTextHistories.asp?historyid=ac02.

HonusWagner.com. "Honus Wagner Biography." Accessed September 12, 2012. http://www.honuswagner.com/biography.html.

Hundhausen, Arthur. "Remember the ABA." Accessed September 18, 2012. http://www.remembertheaba.com.

Hutchins, Robert. "College Football is an Infernal Nuisance." *SI Vault: Sports and Entertainment Digital Network: October 18, 1954*. Accessed September 22, 2012. http://sportsillustrated.cnn.com/vault/article/magazine/MAG1128811/4/index.htm.

Lahanas, Michael. "Hercules and the Olympic Games." *Hellenica, Information about Greece and Cyprus*. Accessed September 16, 2012. http://www.mlahanas.de/Greeks/HerculesOlympics.htm.

Leifer, Neil. "Neil Leifer Photography." Accessed September 23, 2012. http://216.117.181.169/biography.html.

Little League Online. "Dennis Lewin Assumes Chairmanship of Little League International Board of Directors." Accessed September 22, 2012. http://www.littleleague.org/media/newsarchive/2007stories/2007_boardofdirectors.htm.

Little League Online. "Little League Chronology." Accessed September 22, 2012. http://www.littleleague.org/learn/about/historyandmission/chronology.htm.

Los Angeles Times. "Grantland Rice – Hollywood Star Walk." Accessed September 15, 2012. http://projects.latimes.com/hollywood/star-walk/grantland-rice/.

Martin, Douglas. "Steve Sabol, 69, Creative Force Behind NFL Films, Dies." *The New York Times Online*. Accessed September 24, 2012. http://www.nytimes.

com/2012/09/19/sports/football/steve-sabol-creative-force-behind-nfl-films-dies-at-69.html?_r=2&emc=eta1&pagewanted=all.

Masters, James. "Lawn and Real Tennis." *The Online Guide to Traditional Games*. Accessed September 19, 2012. http://www.tradgames.org.uk/games/Tennis.htm.

Maurer School of Law: Indiana University. "Federal Communications Law Journal 47, 3 Cox." Accessed September 23, 2012. http://www.law.indiana.edu/fclj/pubs/v47/no3/cox.html.

McKay, Brett, and Kate McKay. "Boxing: A Manly History of the Sweet Science of Bruising."

The Art of Manliness. Accessed October 1, 2012. http://artofmanliness.com/2009/05/30/boxing-a-manly-history-of-the-sweet-science-of-bruising/.

Media History Project: University of Minnesota. "Media History Project." Accessed September 28, 2012. http://www.mediahistory.umn.edu/timeline/1600-1699.html.

Miklich, Eric. "Baseball History: 19th Century Baseball." Accessed September 29, 2012. http://www.19cbaseball.com/.

Museum of Broadcast Communications. "Sports and Television." Accessed October 21, 2012. http://www.museum.tv/eotvsection.php?entrycode=sportsandte.

The New York Times. "Ring Lardner Dies; Noted as Writer." Accessed September 16, 2012. http://www.nytimes.com/learning/general/onthisday/bday/0306.html.

NFLFootballHistory.net. "NFL in the 1970s." Accessed September 25, 2012. http://www.nflfootballhistory.net/70.htm.

Olympic.org. "Pierre de Coubertin." Accessed September 16, 2012. http://www.olympic.org/content/museum/Mosaic/Sport-equipment/Pierre-de-Coubertin/.

Ours, Robert. "Introduction: A Brief History on College Football." *College Football Encyclopedia*. Accessed October 7, 2012. http://www.footballencyclopedia.com/cfeintro.htm.

Pan, Wendy. "A Short History of Sports Photography." Accessed September 23, 2012. http://ezinearticles.com/?A-Short-History-of-Sports-Photography&id=1572688.

Pickert, Kate. "A Brief History of the X Games." *TIME*.com. Accessed September 15, 2012. http://www.time.com/time/nation/article/0%2C8599%2C1873166%2C00.html.

Pro Football Hall of Fame. "History: The First Televised Game." Accessed October 2, 2012. http://www.profootballhof.com/history/decades/1930s/first_televised_game.aspx.

Pro Football Hall of Fame. "History Release » Football Firsts." Accessed September 30, 2012. http://www.profootballhof.com/history/release.aspx?release_id=1476.

Raney, Arthur A., and Jennings Bryant. Handbook of Sports and Media. New York: Routledge, 2006.

Rowe, David. *Critical Readings: Sport, Culture, and the Media*. Berkshire, England: Open University Press, 2004.

Rudd, David. "A Brief History of Baseball Cards." *Cycleback.com: Center for Artifact Studies*. Accessed October 17, 2012. http://www.cycleback.com/1800s/briefhistory.htm.

Sapercom LLC. "The History of College Football." Accessed September 23, 2012. http://www.historyoffootball.net/history_of_college_football.html.

Sapercom LLC. "The History of Football." Accessed September 23, 2012. http://www. historyoffootball.net/history_of_football.html.

Sapercom LLC. "History of the Game of Basketball." Accessed September 20, 2012. http://www.historyofbasketball.net/.

Spartacus Educational. "Pierre de Coubertin." Accessed September 17, 2012. http://www.spartacus.schoolnet.co.uk/SPOcoubertin.htm.

Straubhaar, Joseph D., Robert LaRose, and Lucinda Davenport. *Media Now: Understanding Media, Culture, and Technology*. Belmont, CA: Thomson/Wadsworth, 2012.

Texas State University Department of Health and Human Performance. "Beginning of Organized Sports in America." Accessed October 9, 2012. http://www.hhp.txstate.edu/hper/faculty/pankey/1310/ch17Bread.htm.

The Tennis Channel. "About Us." *Tennis Channel: Home of the Slams*. Aired September 26, 2012.

Topend Sports. "A Football History - From Its Origin to Now." Accessed September 17, 2012. http://www.topendsports.com/sport/soccer/history.htm.

United States Golf Association. "The Official Site of the U.S. Open Championship Conducted by the USGA – U.S. Open, 2008." Accessed September 27, 2012. http://usga.usopen.com/history/index.html.

USA Network. "US Open Tennis Championship Tournament Coverage, Leaderboard Results,

TV Schedule - USA Network -History." Accessed September 26, 2012. http://www.usanetwork.com/sports/usopen/theshow/history/history.html.

Wenner, Lawrence A. *Media, Sports, & Society*. Newbury Park, CA: Sage Publications, 1989.

Chap. 3: History of the Olympics

Beliefnet.com. "Top 15 Most Inspirational Olympic Moments." *Beliefnet.com*. Accessed October 26, 2012. http://www.beliefnet.com/Entertainment/2008/09/Top-15-Most-Inspirational-Olympic-Moments.aspx?b=1&p=6.

British Library. "Landmarks in the history of the media and the Olympics." *Sport & Society: The Summer Olympics through the lens of social science*. Accessed October 26, 2012. http://www.bl.uk/sportandsociety/exploresocsci/sportsoc/media/articles/landmarks.pdf.

Bureau of Public Affairs: United States Department of State. "Milestones: The Olympic Boycott." Accessed October 29, 2012. http://history.state.gov/milestones/1977-1980/Olympic.

Encyclopedia Britannica Online. "Olympic Games." Accessed September 19, 2012. http://www.britannica.com/EBchecked/topic/428005/Olympic-Games.

Encyclopedia Britannica Online. "Pankration." Accessed September 14, 2012. http://www.britannica.com/EBchecked/topic/440968/pankration.

History.com "First Winter Olympics – This Day in History 1/25/1924." Accessed October 26, 2012. http://www.history.com/this-day-in-history/first-winter-olympics.

Museum.TV. "Olympics and Television." *Museum of Broadcast Communication.* Accessed October 28, 2012. http://www.museum.tv/eotvsection.php?entrycode=olympicsand.

Olympics.org. "Olympic Games Medals, Results, Sports, Athletes – London 2012 Olympics." Accessed October 26, 2012. http://www.olympic.org.

Olympic.org. "Pierre de Coubertin." Accessed September 16, 2012. http://www.olympic.org/content/museum/Mosaic/Sport-equipment/Pierre-de-Coubertin/.

Scholastic.com. "Origin and History of the Olympic Games" Accessed October 27, 2012. http://teacher.scholastic.com/activities/athens_games/history.htm.

Chap. 4: International Sports

Big Pond Services. "AFL explained." *The official site of the Australian Football League.* Accessed October 14, 2012. http://www.afl.com.au/afl%20explained/tabid/10294/default.aspx.

Bird, Beverly. "Mexican History of Soccer." *Livestrong.com.* Accessed October 21, 2012. http://www.livestrong.com/article/366728-mexican-history-of-soccer/.

Encyclopedia Britannica Online. "Australian rules football (sport)." Accessed October 16, 2012. http://www.britannica.com/EBchecked/topic/44079/Australian-rules-football.

ESPN Cricinfo. "A brief history of cricket." Accessed October 16, 2012. http://www.espncricinfo.com/ci/content/story/239757.html#resource.

FIFA.com. "History of Football – The Global Growth." Accessed October 20, 2012. http://www.fifa.com/classicfootball/history/game/historygame4.html.

GAA.ie. "Hurling." Accessed October 16, 2012. http://www.gaa.ie/about-the-gaa/our-games/hurling/.

IndianTwenty20.com. "Twenty20: Past, Present and Future." Accessed October 15, 2012. http://www.indiatwenty20.com/twenty20-history.htm.

Lacrosse-Information. "Native American Lacrosse." Accessed October 15, 2012. http://www.lacrosse-information.com/native-american-lacrosse.html.

Land, James. "Ideas on Increased TV Coverage for College Lacrosse in College Beat 138." *LAX News.* Accessed October 14, 2012. http://laxnews.com/modules.php?name=News&file=article&sid=449.

MrMike.com. "The History of Horse Racing." *Mike Parker ABR, CRS, GRI, SRES - Greater Cincinnati & Northern Kentucky Real Estate & Relocation.* Accessed October 14, 2012. http://www.mrmike.com/explore/hrhist.htm.

OfficialGamePuck.com "National Hockey League." Accessed October 16, 2012. http://www.officialgamepuck.com/National%20Hockey%20League%20Game/Fox%20Trax.htm#.

Patskou, Paul. "Hockey Night in Canada." *Sports on Radio and Television*. Canadian Communications Foundation. Accessed October 12, 2012. http://www.broadcasting-history.ca/index3.html?url=http%3A//www.broadcasting-history.ca/sportsonradioandtv/HNIC_TV.html.

Randall, Charles. "History of Cricket on TV." *The Telegraph*. Telegraph Media Group LLC. Accessed October 12, 2012. http://www.telegraph.co.uk/sport/cricket/2392937/History-of-cricket-on-TV.html.

Sapercom LLC. "The History of Hockey: The Early Years." Accessed October 12, 2012. http://www.historyofhockey.net/national_hockey_association.html.

Soccer365.com. "September 16: First Live Televised Soccer Match." Accessed October 19, 2012. http://www.soccer365.com/today_in_history/62.

Spartacus Educational Publishers. "The Encyclopedia of British Football." Accessed October 21, 2012. http://www.spartacus.schoolnet.co.uk/Ftelevision.htm.

Spartacus Educational Publishers. "Football League." Accessed October 21, 2012. http://www.spartacus.schoolnet.co.uk/Fleague.htm.

SportsPolo.com. "History of the Equestrian Sport of Polo." Accessed October 13, 2012. http://www.sportpolo.com/history/default.

ThePeopleHistory.com. "History of Association Football (Soccer) – From Early Beginnings to Present." Accessed October 22, 2012. http://www.thepeoplehistory.com/soccerhistory.html.

Chap. 5: Racial Barriers

The Eagle Online. "African-Americans' Rich History in Sports." Accessed November 9, 2012. http://eagle.ceu.edu/article/african-americans-rich-history-sports.

Encyclopedia Britannica Online. "Jack Johnson (American boxer)." Accessed November 10, 2012. http://www.britannica.com/EBchecked/topic/305329/Jack-Johnson.

Evans Jr., Arthur S. "Blacks as Key Functionaries: A Study of Racial Stratification in Professional Sport." *Journal of Black Studies* 28.1 (1997): 43-59.

Fuller, Linda K. *Sportscasters/Sportscasting: Principles and Practices*. New York, New York: Routledge, 2008.

Gettings, John. "Civil Disobedience: Black Medalists raise fists for Civil Rights Movement." Memorable Olympic Moments. Accessed November 10, 2012. http://www.infoplease.com/spot/summer-olympics-mexico-city.html.

IvyLeagueSports.com. "The Ivy Influence: William Henry Lewis." *The History of the Ivy League*. Accessed November 10, 2012. http://www.ivyleaguesports.com/history/blackhistory/2011 12/william_henry_lewis.

Kidzwolrd. "Sports Moments in Black History." Accessed November 4, 2012. http://www.kidzworld.com/article/3081-sports-moments-in-black-history#.

National Museum of American History. "Sports: Breaking Records, Breaking Barriers | Smithsonian's National Museum of American History." Accessed November 8, 2012. http://amhistory.si.edu/sports/exhibit/introduction/index.cfm.

Ross, Charles K. *Race and Sport: The Struggle for Equality on and off the Field*. Jackson, Mississippi: University Press of Mississippi, 2005.

Rowe, David. *Critical Readings: Sport, Culture, and the Media*. Berkshire, England: Open University Press, 2004.

Timetoast. "African Americans in Sports History Timeline." Accessed November 6, 2012. http://www.timetoast.com/timelines/african-americans-in-sports-history.

Utah State University. "African-Americans' Rich History in Sports." *The Eagle Online: The Voice of Utah State University – College of Eastern Utah*. Accessed November 9, 2012. http://eagle.ceu.edu/article/african-americans-rich-history-sports.

Wenner, Lawrence A. *Media, Sports, & Society*. Newbury Park, CA: Sage Publications, 1989.

Chap. 6: Women in Sport

AAGPBL.org. "League History." Accessed November 17, 2012. http://www.aagpbl.org/index.cfm/pages/league/12/league-history.

Acosta, R. Vivian and Carpenter, Linda J. "Women in sport." In Donald Chu, Jeffrey O. Segrave & Beverly J. Becker, eds. *Sport and Higher Education*. (Champaign, IL: Human Kinetics, 1985), 313-325.

Bertine, Kathryn. "Kathryn 'Tubby' Johnston in a league of her own." *ESPN: Women*. ESPN Internet Ventures, Accessed November 16, 2012. http://espn.go.com/espnw/features-profiles/6430990/kathryn-tubby-johnston-league-own.

ESPN.com. "Billie Jean King – Title IX: Top 40 Female Athletes." Accessed November 19, 2012. http://espn.go.com/espnw/title-ix/top-40-female-athletes/_/num/31.

ESPN.com. "The First Fabulous Sports Babe." Accessed November 18, 2012. http://espn.go.com/sportscentury/features/00014149.html.

ESPN.com "History of the FIFA Women's World Cup." Accessed November 14, 2012. http://soccernet.espn.go.com/feature?id=454056&cc=5901.

Festle, Mary Jo. *Playing Nice: Politics and Apologies in Women's Sports*. New York: Columbia University Press, 1996.

Gerber, Ellen W., Felshin, Jan., Berlin, Pearl., and Wyrick, Waneen., eds. *The American Woman in Sport*. Reading, MA: Addison-Wesley, 1974.

Hoffarth, Tom. "Title IX 40 Years Later: Broadcasters continue to give a voice to the legacy." *LA Daily News*. Los Angeles Newspaper Group. Accessed November 22, 2012. http://www.dailynews.com/sportscolumnists/ci_20913923/title-ix-40-years-later-broadcasters-lend-voices.

Homer. *The Odyssey of Homer*. Allen Mandelbaum, trans. Berkeley, CA: University of California Press, 1990.

Hultstrand, Bonnie J. "The Growth of Collegiate Women's Sports: The 1960s." *The Journal of Physical Education, Recreation, and Dance*, 64.3 (1993): 41-43.

Hult, Joan S. "The story of women's athletics: Manipulating a dream 1890-1985." In D.M. Costa & S.R. Guthrie, eds., *Women and Sport: Interdisciplinary perspectives*. (Champaign, IL: Human Kinetics, 1994), 83-107.

Lucas, J.A., and R.A. Smith. "Women's Sport: A trial of equality." In R. Howell, ed., *Her Story in Sport: A Historical Anthology of Women in Sports*. (West Point, NY: Leisure Press, 1982), 239-265.

NWLC.org. "Faces of Title IX." Accessed November 17, 2012. http://www.nwlc.org/title-ix/julia-chase.

Park, Roberta J., and Joan S. Hult. "Women as Leaders in Physical Education and School-Based Sports, 1865 to the 1930s." *The Journal of Physical Education, Recreation & Dance*, 64.3 (1993): 35-40.

Rodriguez III, Gene. "History of Women's Golf." *Articles and Answers about Life*. Life 123, Inc. Accessed November 16, 2012. http://www.life123.com/sports/golf-tennis/golf-rules/womens-golf.shtml.

Schubert, Arline F., George W. Schubert, and Cheryl L. Schubert-Madsen. "Changes Influenced by Litigation in Women's Intercollegiate Athletics." *Seton Hall Journal of Sport Law*, 1 (1991): 237-268.

Schwartz, Larry. "Billie Jean Won for All Women." *ESPN.com*. Accessed November 18, 2012. http://espn.go.com/sportscentury/features/00016060.html.

Sperber, Murray A. *College sports Inc.: The Athletic Department vs. the University*. New York: John Hopkins Press, 1990.

Sports Illustrated. "The Most Influential People in Title IX History." *Sports Illustrated: SI.com*.

Time Inc. Accessed November 16, 2012. http://sportsillustrated.cnn.com/multimedia/photo_gallery/0706/gallery.title.IX/content.1.html.

Stern, Robert N. "The Development of an Inter-Organizational Control Network: The case of intercollegiate athletics." *Administrative Science Quarterly*, 24 (1979): 242-266.

TitleIX.info. "History of Title IX." Accessed November 17, 2012. http://www.titleix.info/Faces-of-Title-IX/Faces-Of-Title-IX-Overview.aspx.

Thelin, John R. *Games Colleges Play: Scandal and Reform in Intercollegiate Athletics*. Baltimore, MD: John Hopkins University Press, 1994.

WNBA.com. "MERCURY: Q&A with Billie Jean King." Accessed November 19, 2012. http://www.wnba.com/mercury/news/billiejean_qa_120217.html.

Chap. 7: Amateur Athletics in the United States

Baseball-Almanac.com "World Series History." Accessed January 12, 2013. http://www.baseball-almanac.com/ws/wsmenu.shtml.

Billings, Andrew C. "Dueling Genders: Announcer bias in the 1999 U.S. Open Tennis Tournament." In Robert S. Brown and Daniel J. O'Rourke, eds. *Case Studies in Sport Communication.* (Westport, CT: Praeger, 2003), 51-62.

Billingsley, Richard. "The Road to the BCS has been a long one." *ESPN.com.* Accessed January 10, 2013. http://assets.espn.go.com/ncf/s/historybcs.html.

De Moraes, Lisa. "Super Bowl XLVI: Biggest TV Audience Ever." *The Washington Post.* Accessed January 14, 2013. http://www.washingtonpost.com/blogs/tv-column/post/super-bowl-xlvi-no-tv-ratings-record/2012/02/06/gIQAVAD6tQ_blog.html.

Deadline.com. "March Madness: NCAA Tourney Takes Best Rating in 18 Years." Accessed January 9, 2013. http://www.deadline.com/2012/03/march-madness-ncaa-tourney-takes-best-ratings-in-18-years-report/.

Enberg, Dick with Jim Perry. *Oh my!* Champaign, IL: Sports Publishing, 2004.

Fuller, Linda K. *Sportscasters/Sportscasting: Principles and Practices.* New York, New York: Routledge, 2008.

Gifford, Frank with Harry Waters. *The Whole Ten Yards.* New York: Random House, 1993.

Hauser, Melanie. "Golf." In Abraham Aamidor, ed. *Real sports reporting.* (Bloomington, IN: Indiana University Press, 2003).

Hedrick, Tom. *The Art of Sportscasting: How to build a successful career.* South Bend, IN: Diamond Communications, 2000.

Klein, Christopher. "A Brief History of College Bowl Games." *History in the Headlines.* A&E Television Networks, LLC. Accessed January 12, 2013. http://www.history.com/news/a-brief-history-of-college-bowl-games.

Koebler, Jason. "High School Sports Participation Increases for 22nd Straight Year." USNews.com. Accessed July 12, 2013. http://www.usnews.com/education/blogs/high-school-notes/2011/09/02/high-school-sports-participation-increases-for-22nd-straight-year.

McChesney, Robert W. "Media Made Sport: A history of sports coverage in the United States." In Lawrence A. Wenner, ed. *Media, Sports, & Society.* (Newbury Park, CA: Sage, 19898), 49-69.

NCAA.com. "Celebrating 75 Years of March Madness." Accessed January 11, 2013. http://www.ncaa.com/march-madness.

Newcomb, Tim. "The 2012 Super Bowl, by the Numbers." *Time Newsfeed.* Time, Inc. Accessed January 10, 2013. http://newsfeed.time.com/2012/02/02/the-2012-super-bowl-by-the-numbers/.

O'Donnell, Lewis B., Carl Hausman, and Philip Benoit. *Announcing: Broadcast Communications Today,* 2nd ed. Belmont, CA: Wadsworth, 1992.

Real, Michael. "Sports Online: The newest player in mediasport." In Arthur A. Raney and Jennings Bryant, eds. *Handbook of Sports and Media.* (Mahwah, NJ: Lawrence Erlbaum, 2006), 171-184.

Chap. 8: Sports Media Ethics

Allan, Stuart. *The Routledge Companion to News and Journalism*. Abingdon, Oxon: Routledge, 2010.

Andrews, Phil. *Sports Journalism: A Practical Guide*. London: Sage, 2005

Bender, Gary with Michael L. Johnson. *Call of the game: What really goes on in the broadcast booth*. Chicago, IL: Bonus Books, 1994.

Bender, John R., Lucinda D. Davenport, Michael W. Drager, and Fred Fedler. *Reporting for the Media*. New York: Oxford University Press, 2012.

Berman, Len. *Spanning the World: The Crazy Universe of Big Time Sports, All-Star Egos, and Hall of Fame Bloopers*. New York: William Morrow, 2005.

Carey, Mike with Jamie Most. *High Above Courtside: The Lost Memoirs of Johnny Most*. Champaign, IL: Sports Publishing, 2003.

Durslag, Melvin. "I Don't Care Who Wins, as Long as We Do!: An unblushing defense of announcers who root for the home team." *TV Guide*, May 17, 1999.

Fuller, Linda K. *Sportscasters/Sportscasting: Principles and Practices*. New York, New York: Routledge, 2008.

Gibson, Roy. *Radio and television reporting*. Boston, MA: Allyn and Bacon, 1991.

Hitchcock, John R. *Sportscasting*. Boston, MA: Focal Press, 1991.

McKay, Jim. *My Wide World*. New York: Macmillan Publishing Co., 1973.

Real, Michael R. "Super Bowl: Mythic Spectacle." *Journal of Communication* 25.1 (1975): 31-43.

Rowe, David. *Critical Readings: Sport, Culture, and the Media*. Berkshire, England: Open University Press, 2004.

Schultz-Jorgensen, S. "The World's Best Advertising Agency: The Sports Press," *International*

Sports Press Survey 2005. Copenhagen: House of Monday Morning: Play the Game. Accessed January 17, 2013. http://www.playthegame.org/upload/sport_press_survey_english.pdf, 2005.

Wenner, Lawrence A. *Media, Sports, & Society*. Newbury Park, CA: Sage Publications, 1989.

Whittle, J. *Bad Blood: The Secret Life of the Tour de France*. London: Yellow Jersey Press, 2008.

Wulfemeyer, Tim. "Ethics in Sports Journalism: Tightening up the code." *Journal of Mass Media Ethics* 1.1 (1985): 57–67

Chap. 9: The Business Side of Sports

Academy of Television Arts & Sciences. "ABC's Wide World of Sports." Accessed February 24, 2013. http://www.emmytvlegends.org/interviews/shows/abc-s-wide-world-of-sports.

Aschoff, Edward. "SEC will distribute $289.7 million in revenue." *ESPN.com.* Accessed August 11, 2013. http://espn.go.com/blog/ncfnation/post/_/id/79273/sec-will-distribute-289-7-million-in-revenue.

Aschoff, Edward. "SEC to distribute $289.4 million." *ESPN.com.* Accessed August 11, 2013. http://espn.go.com/college-sports/story/_/id/9329603/sec-schools-receive-207-million-conference.

Barnett, Steven. *Games and sets: The changing face of sport on television.* London: BFI Publishing, 1990.

Carter, David M. *Keeping score: An Inside Look at Sports Marketing.* Grants Pass, OR: The Oasis Press, 1996.

CollegeFootballUniverseBlog.com. "Television revenue for top collegiate conferences skyrocket, do schools need the money?" Accessed August 7, 2013. http://www.collegefootballuniverseblog.com/1/post/2012/12/television-revenue-for-top-collegiate-conferences-skyrocket-do-schools-need-the-money.html.

Conrad, Mark. *The Business of Sports: A Primer for Journalists.* New York, NY: Routledge, 2009.

Correy, S. "Who Plays on Pay?" *Media Information Australia,* 1995.

Deitsch, Richard. "NFL, networks win in extended rights deal." *SI.com* 23 Feb 2013. http://sportsillustrated.cnn.com/2011/writers/richard_deitsch/12/15/nfl.rights.deal/index.html.

Dosh, Kristi. "Texas tops in football profit, revenue." *ESPN.com.* Accessed August 11, 2013. http://espn.go.com/blog/playbook/dollars/post/_/id/2556/texas-tops-in-football-profit-revenue.

ESPN.com. "College Athletics Revenues and Expenses – 2008." Accessed August 12, 2013. http://espn.go.com/ncaa/revenue.

ESPN.com. "Five Minutes Away from Never." Accessed February 23, 2013. http://espn.go.com/abcsports/wwos/rarledge.html.

Encyclopedia Britannica Online. "Television in the United States: The Development of Sports Programming." Accessed February 25, 2013. http://www.britannica.com/EBchecked/topic/1576618/ABCs-Wide-World-of-Sports.

Forbes.com. "NFL Team Values – The Business of Football." Accessed August 14, 2013. http://www.forbes.com/nfl-valuations/list/.

Gaines, Cork. "NFL Players And Owners Are Fighting Over The Biggest Pie In Sports." *BusinessInsider.com.* Accessed August 12, 2013. http://www.businessinsider.com/nfl-biggest-pie-in-sports-2011-3.

Goldlust, J. *Playing for Keeps: Sport, the Media, and Society.* Melbourne: Longman Cheshire, 1987.

Gotthelf, Josh. *"Linebacker: Agent Paid Me Cash."* SportBusiness Journal 1 (July 26, 1999).

Heitner, Darren. "Billy Hunter's Lawsuit Against Derek Fisher And The NBPA Could Be Worth Millions Of Dollars." *Forbes.com.* Accessed August 18, 2013. http://www.forbes.com/sites/darrenheitner/2013/05/19/billy-hunters-lawsuit-against-derek-fisher-and-the-nbpa-could-be-worth-millions-of-dollars/.

Hoffer, Richard. "What a Wonderful World: Debuting 50 Years ago, Wide World of Sports changed the game." *SI Vault*. Turner Sports & Entertainment Digital Network. Accessed February 25, 2013. http://sportsillustrated.cnn.com/vault/article/magazine/MAG1185032/index.htm.

Lee, Soonhwan and Hyosung Chun. "Economic Values of Professional Sport Franchises in the United States." *The Sport Journal*. Accessed February 21, 2013. http://www.thesport-journal.org/article/economic-values-professional-sport-franchises-united-states.

Levinson, David and Karen Christensen. *Berkshire Encyclopedia of World Sport*. Berkshire Publishing Group: Great Barrington, MA, 2005.

Leeds, Michael and Peter von Allmen. *The Economics of Sports*. Pearson Education, Inc., 2005.

Maske, Mark. "NFL completes TV deal with Fox, CBS and NBC totaling about $3 billion per year." *WashingtonPost.com*. Accessed August 16, 2013. http://articles.washington-post.com/2011-12-14/sports/35285272_1_night-games-new-tv-deals-nfl-network.

Museum.TV. "National Broadcasting Company: U.S. Network." *The Museum of Broadcast Communications*. Accessed February 24, 2013. http://www.museum.tv/eotvsection.php?entrycode=nationalbroa.

Museum of Broadcast Communications. "Olympics and Television." Accessed February 23, 2013. http://www.museum.tv/eotvsection.php?entrycode=olympicsand.

Museum of Broadcast Communications. "Roone Arledge: U.S. Media Producer/Executive." Accessed February 21, 2013. http://www.museum.tv/eotvsection.php?entrycode=arledgeroon.

NBCSports.com. "The History of the NFL on NBC." *Super Bowl XLVI Media Guide*. Accessed February 20, 2013. http://press.nbcsports.com/docs/history-of-the-nfl-on-nbc.html.

Olenski, Steve. "The Power of Global Sports Brand Merchandising." *Forbes*. Forbes.com LLC. Accessed February 3, 2013. http://www.forbes.com/sites/marketshare/2013/02/06/the-power-of-global-sports-brand-merchandising/.

Peloquin, Matt. "2012 NCAA Television Revenue by Conference." *CollegeSportsInfo.com*. Accessed August 7, 2013. http://collegesportsinfo.com/2012/05/10/2012-ncaa-television-revenue-by-conference/.

Rader, Benjamin G. *American sports: From the Age of Folk Games to the Age of Televised Sports*. Upper Saddle River, NJ: Prentice Hall, Inc., 1999.

Rittenberg, Adam. "B1G revenue, expenses among highest." *ESPN.com* Accessed August 14, 2013. http://espn.go.com/blog/ncfnation/post/_/id/78782/b1g-revenue-expenses-among-highest.

Rowe, David. *Sport, Culture, and the Media*. Philadelphia: Open University Press, 1999.

Smith, Anthony F. with Keith Hollihan. *ESPN the Company: The Story and Lessons Behind the Most Fanatical Brand in Sports*. John Wiley & Sons, New Jersey, 2009.

Smith, Chris. "College Football's Most Valuable Teams." *Forbes.com*. Accessed August 10, 2013. http://www.forbes.com/sites/chrissmith/2011/12/22/college-footballs-most-valuable-teams/.

Smith, Chris. "The Most Valuable Conferences in College Sports." *Forbes.com*. Accessed August 10, 2013. http://www.forbes.com/sites/chrissmith/2013/01/16/the-most-valuable-conferences-in-college-sports/.

Shropshire, Kenneth L. and Timothy Davis. *The Business of Sports Agents*. University of Pennsylvania Press: Philadelphia, 2003.

SportsBusinessDaily.com. "The 20 Most Influential Sports Agents." Accessed February 22, 2013. http://www.sportsbusinessdaily.com/Journal/Issues/2008/08/20080818/SBJ-In-Depth/The-20-Most-Influential-Sports-Agents.aspx.

Steinberg, Leigh. *"Time to Revise Game Rules."* Sporting News 10: (November 16, 1987).

USAToday.com. "Top School Revenue." Accessed August 11, 2013.http://www.usatoday.com/sports/college/schools/finances/.

Chap. 10: Sports Agents, Endorsements, and Advertising

AthletePromotions.com. "Athlete Product Endorsements, Hire an Athlete for an Endorsement." *Sports Speakers Bureau Booking Athlete Appearances*. Accessed February 25, 2013. http://www.athletepromotions.com/athlete-product-endorsements.php.

Belzer, Jason. "The World's Most Valuable Sports Agencies." *Forbes.com*. Accessed August 19, 2013. http://www.forbes.com/sites/jasonbelzer/2013/06/24/the-worlds-most-valuable-sports-agencies-2/.

Biderman, David. "The Stadium-Naming Game: Some Companies Score Big Wins with Sponsorship, as Others See the Home Team Flop." *The Wall Street Journal*. Accessed February 22, 2013. http://online.wsj.com/article/SB10001424052748704022804575041493468426912.html.

Boyle, Raymond. *Sports Journalism: Context and Issues*. London: Sage, 2006.

Broughton, David. "Sports ad spending roars back." *SportsBusinessDaily.com*. Accessed August 16, 2013. http://www.sportsbusinessdaily.com/Journal/Issues/2011/05/02/Research-and-Ratings/Ad-spending.aspx.

Broughton, David. "Verizon tops among ad spenders." *SportsBusinessDaily.com*. Accessed August 16, 2013. http://www.sportsbusinessdaily.com/Journal/Issues/2012/06/04/Research-and-Ratings/Ad-spending.aspx.

CBSSports.com. "MLB Salaries." Accessed August 17, 2013. http://www.cbssports.com/mlb/salaries/avgsalaries.

Chip Ganassi Racing. "Chevron Texaco signs NASCAR Winston Cup contest with Chip Ganassi Racing w/ Felix Sabates." Accessed March 14, 2013. http://www.chipganassiracingwithfelixsabates.com/cgi-bin/ db_searchz.cgi?user_id=94619&database=dbpg_teamnews. exm&template=tmplt_teamnews_sr2.htm&0=136928.

Conrad, Mark. *The Business of Sports: A Primer for Journalists*. New York: Lawrence Erlbaum Associates, Inc., 2006.

ESPN.com. "Super Bowl just shy of TV record." Accessed August 10, 2013. http://espn. go.com/nfl/playoffs/2012/story/_/id/8913211/2013-super-bowl-falls-short-television-ratings-record.

TheFiscalTimes.com. "How Corporations Sponsor Olympic Athletes." *Business + Economy.*

The Fiscal Times, Accessed September 20, 2012. http://www.thefiscaltimes.com/ Articles/2012/08/08/How-Corporations-Sponsor-Olympic-Athletes.aspx#page1.

Fisher, Robert and Kirk Wakefield. "Factors Leading to Group Identification: A Field Study of Winners and Losers." *Psychology and Marketing* 15 (1998): 23-44.

Goetzl, David. "TV Ad Spending Appears To Pass $70 Billion for the First Time, Sports Spending Also Growing." *MediaPost.com.* Accessed August 16, 2013. http://www. mediapost.com/publications/article/173472/tv-ad-spending-appears-to-pass-70-bil-lion-for-the.html.

Goldman, Leah and Dashiell Bennett. "12 Athlete Endorsements that were Lost to Scandal." *Business Insider.* Accessed February 15, 2013. http://www.businessinsider. com/12-athlete-endorsements-that-were-lost-to-scandal-2011-8?op=1.

Gwinner, Kevin P. and John Eaton. "Building Brand Image through Event Sponsorship: The role of image transfer." *Journal of Advertising* 28.4 (1999): 47-57.

Gwinner, Kevin P. and John Eaton. "A Model of Image Creation and Image Transfer in Event Sponsorship." *International Marketing Review* 14.3 (1997): 145-158.

Haynes, Richard and Raymond Boyle. *Power Play: Sport, the Media, and Popular Culture.* Ediburgh: Edinburgh University Press, 2009.

Hof, Robert. "Online Ad Revenues to Pass Print in 2012." *Forbes.com.* Accessed August 11, 2013. http://www.forbes.com/sites/roberthof/2012/01/19/ online-ad-revenues-to-pass-print-in-2012/.

IAB.net. "Internet Ad Revenues Again Hit Record-Breaking Double-Digit Annual Growth, Reaching Nearly $37 Billion, a 15% Increase Over 2011's Landmark Numbers." Accessed August 12, 2013. http://www.iab.net/about_the_iab/recent_press_releases/ press_release_archive/press_release/pr-041613.

HonusWagner.com. "Honus Wagner Biography." Accessed September 12, 2012. http:// www.honuswagner.com/biography.html.

iSportsConnect.com. "Usain Bolt Tops Athlete Sponsorship Table at London 2012." Accessed March 15, 2013. http://www.isportconnect.com/index.php?option=com_content&vie w=article&id=13629:usain-bolt-tops-athlete-sponsorship-table-at-london-2012&cati d=44:olympics&Itemid=50.

Lefton, Terry. "Pepsi returns to Super Bowl." *SportsBusinessDaily.com.* Accessed August 16, 2013. http://www.sportsbusinessdaily.com/Journal/Issues/2012/06/25/Marketing-and-Sponsorship/Pepsi.aspx.

Madrigal, Robert. "The Influence of Social alliances with Sports Teams on Intentions to Purchase Corporate Sponsors' Products." *Journal of Advertising* 29.4 (2000), 13-24.

MillerCoors.com. "Timeline." Accessed February 25, 2013. http://www.millercoors.com/ Who-We-Are/Timeline.aspx.

Moore, Paula. "Stadium Naming Deals Haven't Hurt Pepsi and Coors." *Denver Business Journal* 52.31 (2001): 22A.

Morgan, Angela and Miyazaki, Anthony. "Assessing Market Value of Event Sponsoring: Corporate Olympic Sponsorships." *Journal of Advertising Research* 41.1 (2000): 9-15.

Morgan, Melissa Jane Johnson, and Jane Summers. *Sports Marketing*. Southbank, Vic.: Thomson, 2005.

NBCNews.com. "Lance Armstrong Steps Down from Livestrong, Loses Nike, Bud Contracts." Accessed February 17, 2013. http://www.nbcnews.com/business/lance-armstrong-steps-down-livestrong-loses-nike-bud-contracts-1C6512991.

Novy-Williams, Eben. "Honus Wagner Card May Sell at Auction for More than $2.8 Millon." *Bloomberg*. Accessed September 12, 2012. http://www.bloomberg.com/news/2013-01-04/honus-wagner-card-may-sell-at-auction-for-more-than-2-8-million.html.

PerformanceResearch.com. "Naming Rights, Naming Wrongs." Accessed March 17, 2013. http://www.performanceresearch.com/stadium-sponsorship.htm.

Rudd, David. "A Brief History of Baseball Cards." *Cycleback.com: Center for Artifact Studies*. Accessed October 17, 2012. http://www.cycleback.com/1800s/briefhistory.htm.

Schaaf, Phil. *Sports, Inc.: 100 Years of Sports Business*. Amherst, NY: Prometheus Books, 2004.

SoccerLens.com. "The World's Biggest Soccer Sponsors." Accessed March 3, 2013. http://soccerlens.com/the-worlds-biggest-soccer-sponsors/52174/.

SportsAgentBlog.com. "Model Rule 15% Fees." Accessed August 19, 2013. http://www.sportsagentblog.com/2007/12/11/model-rule-15-fees/.

SportsIllustrated.com. "$256,296,950." Accessed August 17, 2013. http://sportsillustrated.cnn.com/vault/article/magazine/MAG1065863/index.htm.

Speed, Richard and Peter Thompson. "Determinants of Sports Sponsorship Response." *Journal of the Academy of Marketing Science* 28.2 (2000): 226-238.

Steinberg, Brian. "Who Bought What in Super Bowl 2013: Anheuser Busch to Wonderful Pistachios." *AdAge.com*. Accessed August 15, 2013. http://adage.com/article/special-report-super-bowl/buying-super-bowl-2013/238489/.

Street, Scott. "Have Corporate Sponsor, Will Study." *The Chronicle of Higher Education* 47.4 (2000): A10.

Yahoo! Sports. "How Michael Jordan Still Earns $80 Million A Year." *Yahoo! Sports*. Accessed February 14, 2013. http://sports.yahoo.com/news/michael-jordan-still-earns-80-million-175222679--nba.html.

Chap. 11: Sports Films

Edgington, K. and Thomas L. Erskine with James M. Welsh. *Encyclopedia of Sports Films*. Blue Ridge Summit, PA: Scarecrow Press. 2011.

Reiter, Adam. "15 Best Athletes Who Became Actors." *Bleacher Report, Inc.* 2013. Accessed March 22, 2013. http://bleacherreport.com/articles/814005-15-best-athletes-who-became-actors/page/16.

Chap. 12: Future of Sports Media

Bobbitt, David. "Teaching McLuhan: Understanding Media." *George Mason University.* Accessed July 26, 2013. http://enculturation.gmu.edu/teaching-mcluhan.

ESPN.com. "Love: McHale won't return." Accessed August 19, 2013. http://sports.espn.go.com/nba/news/story?id=4265512.

FoxNews.com. "Dwight Howard tweets that he'll sign with Houston Rockets." Accessed August 26, 2013. http://www.foxnews.com/sports/2013/07/06/dwight-howard-tweets-that-hell-sign-with-rockets/.

Lunden, Ingrid. "Analyst: Twitter Passed 500M Users in June 2012, 140M of Them in US; Jakarta 'Biggest Tweeting' City." *Techcrunch.com.* Accessed August 8, 2013. http://techcrunch.com/2012/07/30/analyst-twitter-passed-500m-users-in-june-2012-140m-of-them-in-us-jakarta-biggest-tweeting-city/a.

Twitter.com. "The Engineering behind Twitter's New Search Experience." Accessed August 21, 2013. https://blog.twitter.com/2011/engineering-behind-twitter%E2%80%99s-new-search-experience.

Image Credits

1. Copyright © 2013 by Depositphotos / scaliger.
2. National Photo Company / Public Domain.
3. ABC Television / Public Domain.
4. National Photo Company / Public Domain.
5. Copyright © 2012 by Depositphotos / everett225.
6. Copyright © 2013 by Depositphotos / jorgefelix.
7. Copyright © 2013 by Depositphotos / jorgefelix.
8. United States Information Agency / Public Domain.
9. Copyright © 2013 by Depositphotos / natursports.
10. Copyright © 2013 by Depositphotos / tammykayphoto.
11. Copyright © 2012 by Depositphotos / gunnar3000.
12. Copyright © 2012 by Depositphotos / Apriori.
13. Copyright © 2010 by Depositphotos / photoworksmedia.
14. Copyright © 2013 by Depositphotos / duha127.
15. Copyright © 2013 by Depositphotos / ericbvd.

CPSIA information can be obtained at www.ICGtesting.com
Printed in the USA
LVOW03s0532300814

401534LV00010B/55/P

9 781631 890703